More GOOD NEWS *for* GREAT DAYS

O.S. HAWKINS

Copyright 2008 O.S. Hawkins

ISBN: 0-9779400-2-0
Dewey Decimal Classification: 332.024-dc22
Subject Heading: 1. RELIGIOUS HOLIDAYS - SERMONS
Printed in the United States of America

Unless otherwise noted, Scripture quotations
are from the Holy Bible, New King James Version.

GuideStone·
Financial Resources

OTHER BOOKS BY O.S. HAWKINS

When Revival Comes
After Revival Comes
Clues to a Successful Life
Where Angels Fear to Tread
Tracing the Rainbow Through the Rain
Revive Us Again
Unmasked!
Jonah: Meeting the God of the Second Chance
Getting Down to Brass Tacks
In Sheep's Clothing
Tearing Down Walls and Building Bridges
Moral Earthquakes and Secret Faults
Rebuilding: It's Never Too Late for a New Beginning
Money Talks: But What Is It Really Saying?
Shields of Brass or Shields of Gold?
Good News for Great Days
Drawing the Net
Culture Shock
High Calling, High Anxiety
The Question of Our Time
The Art of Connecting
GuideStones: Ancient Landmarks
The Pastor's Primer
Antology

D E D I C A T I O N

To each and every God-anointed, God-called pastor

who stands in the sacred desk to open the Book of

God to the people of God each Sunday morning

knowing that those words are still a savor of

life unto life to all who will receive them. Pastor,

keep telling the story, be faithful and true as you

share....More Good News for Great Days.

T A B L E   O F   C O N T E N T S

More GOOD NEWS *for* GREAT DAYS

O.S. HAWKINS

F O R E W O R D

GOOD NEWS IS WELCOME ANY TIME. In a world where so many people are searching for meaning in their lives, there is a hunger to hear an encouraging word. The pulpits of our churches still provide the most wonderful opportunity to dispense this news that has changed lives for two millennia now. The Good News of a loving Savior is what the world is still waiting to hear.

As a pastor for over a quarter of a century, I always looked forward to the "special days" on the Christian calendar. I never lamented the fact that on Easter or Christmas or Mother's Day some would attend who might not be back for a year. I always saw this as an opportunity to share the good news on these great days. In this volume you hold in your hand, the good news is expressed throughout its pages. Whatever the special day may afford, it is our opportunity to tell the old and often repeated story with….More Good News for Great Days.

C H A P T E R   I.

N E W   Y E A R ' S   D A Y

Joshua 3:1-17

"NEW" IS ONE OF THOSE WORDS IN OUR ENGLISH LANGUAGE THAT MOST ALWAYS FINDS THE WELCOME MAT OUT AT OUR HEART'S DOOR AND BRINGS A SMILE TO OUR FACE. In our childhood days there was the joy of having a "new" bicycle or a "new" ball glove. In adolescence there was the joy of a "new" car (at least new to us). As we journeyed through life there was the "new" job, then the "new" house and the "new" baby. For those of us who have come to know the Lord Jesus Christ, by grace through faith, there is the "new" birth along with the promise of a "new" life all provided for us through the "new" covenant accompanied by the "new" commandment. And, as if that were not enough, we live with the promise that later we will have a "new" body and a "new" home called heaven. God is the giver of many wonderful "new" things. He is the God of new beginnings.

We stand now at the door of another new beginning; a new year filled with new possibilities and opportunities. Twelve new months, 52 new weeks, 365 new days, 8,760 new hours, 525,000 new minutes and 31,536,000 new seconds…every one of which is God's gift to us.

For the children of Israel it had been a long journey. Moses had led them out of Egyptian bondage, through the Red Sea's parting, to the portals of the Promised Land at Kadesh Barnea, and then back through the wilderness wanderings for four whole decades and finally, to the eastern bank of Jordan just opposite the land of promise. It was now cross over time, decision time, a time to decide once and for all to go on or be content to stay bogged down with the past. It was "D-Day," time to cross over the Jordan and begin the conquest and possession of their new opportunity. It was truly a day of new beginnings.

There are crossover times in every life, times of transition where, like Joshua, we too "have not passed this way before" *(Joshua 3:4b)*. This was a traumatic time for the Israelites. Moses had led them for a whole generation. They had journeyed together through the mountain tops and the valleys. Quite frankly, they had gotten a bit used to that lifestyle. Our human inclination is to get used to what we know. Change does not come easy for most of us. We get comfortable holding on to the past.

New Year's Day provides us with a crossover moment, an opportunity to step out of our comfort zones and into a new beginning. Crossover times can be caused by all sorts of challenges. For some, it is the death of a loved one that causes us to cross over when we have "not passed that way before." For some, crossover moments can be caused by such things as divorce or disease or discouragement or a myriad of other situations or circumstances.

It is interesting that this phrase, "cross over," appears forty-eight times in the Bible. This idea is woven like a thread through the fabric of scripture. Jesus used it himself when he challenged his disciples to "cross over" to the other side of the lake *(Mark 4:35)*. There are times in our lives that call upon us all to be cross over people, to leave our own comfort zones, step out on faith and cross over. This new year affords us such an opportunity.

As we stand at the brink of this new year, our hearts should be filled with anticipation and challenge. Only God knows what the future holds but our possibilities are limitless. Joshua, though he is dead, still speaks to us today and challenges us to enter the new year in the same way he led his people into their new beginning. As we enter the new year we should do so by being flexible, being focused, being faithful, being futuristic and being fearless.

As we enter this new year we should do so by determining to:

BE FLEXIBLE

"...you have not passed this way before" (Joshua 3:4)

Be flexible. Don't be afraid of change. Change can be your friend and not your foe. For three days the children of Israel camped on the banks of the Jordan River looking across at the Promised Land. For three days they contemplated...many hundreds of thousands of them knowing that crossing that river would mean a change from everything they had ever known. It is strange how comfortable we can all get in our own personal wilderness.

Joshua readily admitted that "we have not passed this way before." Perhaps this fear of the unknown feeds the resistance to change as much as anything. Let's face it…change is hard. To illustrate just lay this book down a moment and fold your hands together as though they were in prayer. Now, move your fingers over just one digit. Yes, change is uncomfortable at first. It doesn't "feel" right.

We have a way of subconsciously conditioning ourselves to resist change and new beginnings. James Belasco wrote an intriguing book entitled *Teaching the Elephant to Dance.* He explained how circus elephants when they are small are shackled by their trainer with heavy chains around their ankles. These chains are then held firm by steel stakes deeply imbedded in the ground. The elephant then stays put. He cannot go past the length of his chain. As the months and years unfold and he grows and becomes huge he has more than adequate strength to pull the stake out of the ground. But he never does! He never leaves the length of his chain because he has been conditioned and therefore change is out of the question. His movement becomes limited simply because of mental conditioning. Like these powerful elephants many of us and many of our churches are "bound" because of conditioned restraints, because we, too, "have not passed this way before."

Being flexible to change is a necessity even if we have not "passed this way before." If there is one thing that can be said about our Lord, it is that He brought about a significant amount of change. He was the consummate change agent. In fact, this is

what gave Him so much trouble with the religious traditionalists of His day. He changed everything, even the day of worship and the way of worship.

Some stand at the banks of their own Jordan on the eve of this new year. You, too, "have not passed this way before." The first characteristic of crossover people is that they are not afraid of change. They face the unknown even when they have not "passed that way before." How? By being flexible.

As we enter the new year we should do so by not just being flexible but by determining to also:

BE FOCUSED

"...when you see the ark of the covenant of the Lord your God and the priests, the Levites bearing it, then you shall set out from your place to go after it." (Joshua 3:3)

Be focused. The Israelites were to keep their eyes on the ark and follow it through the Jordan and into their new beginning. That is very good counsel for us on the eve of a new year and a new beginning.

Time and space do not permit us to adequately describe this religious object that has fascinated men and women for three thousand years and has been the subject of some of the most successful and profitable movies in film history. Even as I type these words there are teams of modern-day explorers

looking for it in various parts of the ancient world still today. The ark was an oblong wooden box, overlaid in solid gold with two golden cherubim on the top with their wings touching over what is called the mercy seat. It contained the tablets of the law, a pot of manna and Aaron's rod that budded. It was placed in the Holy of Holies in the tabernacle in the wilderness and later in the temple in Jerusalem. It was there that God would visit His people on the high, holy Day of Atonement with His Shekinah glory.

The ark was a type, a foreshadow, a picture of the Lord Jesus Christ. On that cross-over day the ark was a sign that God was leading His people. Their job in crossing over was rather simple. They were to keep their eyes on the ark and "go after it." Before this day the Bible always speaks of how the ark was in the "midst" of the people. Now, it was leading them into a new day. They were to keep a distance between themselves and the ark. In fact, verse four indicates the distance was the equivalent of ten football fields in length. Why? So the ark would always be visible to the masses of people. It was so that everyone could keep their eyes focused on the ark...so that there would be nothing between them and the ark. Can you imagine the conversation if those hundreds of thousands of people had crowded up to the ark. One would surely be saying, "Where is the ark?" To which another would reply, "I don't know. I am following you. I thought you were following the ark." "Not me, I haven't seen it in days. I am following the guy in front of me. I thought he was following it!"

Aren't we just like that on occasion? We allow so many "things" or even "people" to get between us and the Lord Jesus. Often we find ourselves trying to follow someone else who we think is following the Lord. How much better as we enter a new year to be focused and keep our own eyes on the Lord. He is the one who provides the path through whatever a new year may hold.

Up until this moment, the people of God had been following a "cloud by day and a pillar of fire by night" while awaiting possession of their promised land. Now, those had been removed and the ark, the picture of our Lord, was to take the place of leadership and lead the way for them. What a beautiful picture of Christ who goes before us to open our way. He stands in the midst of our own rivers until we cross over. As we embark on this new year the Bible calls us to be flexible, to not be afraid of change, and also to be focused, to keep our eyes on the Lord Jesus and let him lead us by His spirit through His word into our new year of new beginnings.

Another important characteristic of crossover people is their determination to:

BE FAITHFUL

"…sanctify yourselves for tomorrow the Lord will do wonders among you." (Joshua 3:5)

Be faithful. As we enter a new year this is a call to commit ourselves to stay pure in mind, motives and morals. In the words of Joshua, "Sanctify yourselves." This Hebrew word we translate

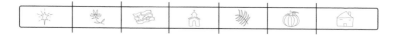

as "sanctify" first appears in scripture in Genesis 2:3 when it says that God "blessed the Sabbath and sanctified it." He separated it from all other days. He set it apart. The new year affords us a new and fresh opportunity to set ourselves apart from the world and recommit ourselves to Christ in faithfulness.

The process of sanctification in the Bible is both positional and progressive. Paul says, "You were washed, you were sanctified, you were justified in the name of the Lord Jesus Christ" *(1 Corinthians 6:11)*. The use of the aorist tense indicates it is something done once and for all. The passive voice that is found here indicates that God did it. At the moment of our salvation God Himself set us apart for Himself. And when we truly know Him then we grow in sanctification by a process of our being continually conformed to His image.

What do you suppose happened that evening as those Israelites camped on the banks of Jordan on the very threshold of all their dreams? They "sanctified themselves." Everyone got right with God. Then what happened? The same thing that always happens when one gets right with God—they got right with each other. People began to show mercy to one another. Forgiveness was in the air they breathed. And love began to flow. By the time Joshua said, "Let's go," they were ready.

Whenever we are faced with new opportunities that can result in new beginnings, God calls upon us to "sanctify ourselves." As we enter this new year let's be flexible and focused, but let's also be faithful by remembering whose we are and by making a renewed commitment to remain pure.

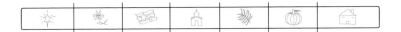

Cross over people also possess a determination to:

BE FUTURISTIC

"…for tomorrow the Lord will work wonders among you."
(Joshua 3:5)

Be futuristic. That is to say on the eve of this new year start believing in tomorrow. For Israel, there was something now for which to look forward. After all those years with no real direction or purpose, now there was hope. Listen to Joshua: "Tomorrow the Lord will work wonders among you!" Hope, faith, vision began to well up within their hearts. They began to believe in tomorrow. They ceased living in the past. Yes, "Tomorrow the Lord will work wonders among you." Thus, as they crossed over, they kept their focus forward and not backward on the past. It was at this point that the Apostle Paul attested that "This one thing I do, forgetting what is behind and reaching forth to those things which are before, I press toward the mark for the high calling of God in Christ Jesus my Lord" *(Philippians 3:13).*

It is a dangerous time in any life, any business, any relationship, or any church, for that matter, when memories of yesterday are more prevalent and important than visions and hopes of tomorrow. Israel had certainly seen her share of miracles in the past. The parting of the Red Sea. The manna which fell each morning. The pillar of fire that appeared each night to lead them. The cloud that hovered by day to point direction. The bitter waters of Marah turning sweet. The water which

flowed from the rock. But now they sat on the banks of the Jordan. It would have been easy to just sit there and reminisce with one another about all they had seen and experienced. But crossover people do not do that. They believe in tomorrow. They trust that "tomorrow the Lord will work wonders among them."

It is a dangerous time in the life of the believer when memories of yesterday are more important than visions of tomorrow. God did not bring you to the bank and brink of a new year for you to just sit and think of what has been in the past. He is affording you a brand new year, another new beginning. Make the best of it. Be flexible. Be focused. Be faithful. And above all be futuristic, believe in tomorrow.

The children of Israel saw not just what had been, or what was, but what was going to be. Crossing the Jordan did not mean that everything was going to be easy on the other side. It wasn't. There was still Jericho. And when they won that battle there were many others to follow in the conquest of the land. But they crossed over with the promise that "tomorrow the Lord will do wonders among us." And did He ever!

A final characteristic of crossover people lies in their determination to:

BE FEARLESS

"…and the Lord said to Joshua, 'This day I will begin to exalt you in the sight of all Israel, that they may know that as I was with Moses, so I will be with you…' " (Joshua 3:3:6-17)

Be fearless. The Israelites had leadership they could trust. They followed Joshua. Why? Because He was God's man and because he provided them with a vision and not a need. He was a fearless leader. They had needs that were many. But this was not their focus.

Joshua led by example. The commitment level rises when men and women see the passion in the one out in front. Joshua's fearless leadership became contagious and the people followed him.

It is important that before the river parted it was the "leaders" who were the first ones to put their feet in the water *(Joshua 3:12-13)*. Leadership is risky business. Many never cross over into new beginnings due to the failure of leaders who are constantly reactive and seldom proactive. The leaders of Israel were to continually hold up the ark so that all could see it and follow.

Fearless leadership and followship won the day. The leader obeyed the Lord. The people heeded the words of the Lord to their leader. Note the words, "And it shall come to pass, as soon as the soles of the feet of the priests who bear the ark of the Lord, the Lord of all the earth, shall rest in the waters of the Jordan, that the waters of the Jordan shall be cut off, the waters that come down from upstream, and they shall stand as a heap" *(Joshua 3:12).* The next phrase simply says, "So it was..." *(Joshua 3:13).* Then we read "...and the people crossed over opposite Jericho" *(Joshua 3:16).* Yes, they became crossover people that day.

I love the final words of the text. "Then the priests who bore the ark of the covenant of the Lord stood firm on dry ground in the midst of the Jordan; and all Israel crossed over on dry ground, until all the people had crossed completely over the Jordan" *(Joshua 3:17)*. This is fearless leadership you can trust. It is no wonder that a few days later when they were instructed to march around the walls of Jericho they did so.

As we stand at the eve of a new year there is a sense in which it is our own Jordan. What shall we do? "We have not passed this way before." How shall we face the new year with its promise of so many new beginnings? The same way that Joshua and his people crossed over to their own new beginning. How? Be flexible. Don't be afraid of change. Be focused. Keep your eyes on the ark, the Lord Jesus. Be faithful. Commit to stay pure in mind, motives and morals. Be futuristic. Believe in tomorrow. And, be fearless. Trust in those around you.

The problem with some of us in taking advantage of new beginnings is that we come to the water's edge and say, "Lord, just let those waters part and then I will step in." But note that it wasn't until "the soles of their feet" touched the water that it parted. It was a step of faith for them…and for us. Often, we have to get our feet wet with faith before God begins to "work wonders among us."

We, like the Israelites of old, have been on our own journey. Now, we are cross-over people ourselves. We are crossing over into a new year with new opportunities and new beginnings.

As we enter this new year, may we, as those who have gone before us, be flexible, be focused, be faithful, be futuristic and, above all, be fearless.

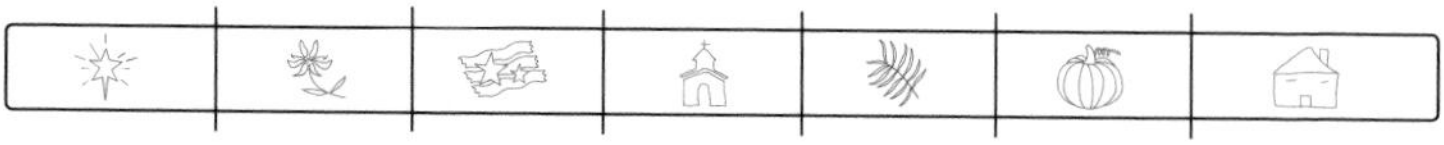

CHAPTER 11.

PALM SUNDAY

Luke 19:28-44

IN OUR HEARTS WE ARE ALL DREAMERS. Most all of us know what it is to dream dreams and see visions of what we might hope to become or what we think would bring happiness and contentment to our lives.

Who of us in our childhood days did not dream of the future? Even as I type these words my mind races back in time to an old vacant lot on Crenshaw Street in east Fort Worth. A thousand times I played ball on that old makeshift diamond and dreamed it was the bottom of the ninth in Yankee Stadium. That old tattered ball with its red threads unraveling was tossed to the plate. The crack of the bat…home run…I could hear the roar of the crowd as I trotted around those bases. As children we were all dreamers at heart. We dreamed of being astronauts, firemen, doctors, ballplayers, and even presidents.

We started college with big dreams of what we were going to do and what we were going to become. We began our careers with dreams of how we were going to advance and where we hoped to be by the time we reached forty (which seemed so long away back then). We started our

marriages with dreams of being the all-American family who would live happily ever after with no heartaches and no problems.

But as the days have extended into weeks, the weeks into months and the months into years many of us have spent much of our time picking up the pieces of broken dreams. Often things do not work out just as we had hoped. Careers don't always develop. Unplanned recessions appear and steal jobs away. Down-sizing can knock on our door at the peak of our earning potential. A husband dies…or leaves. Kids make wrong decisions and bring heartbreak. Yes, broken dreams are no stranger to most of us.

Are there any broken dreams on this Palm Sunday? There were a lot of big dreamers on that first Palm Sunday in Jerusalem. Great crowds had lined the parade route down Palm Sunday Road from the summit of the Mount of Olives down the western slope, through the Kidron Valley, up the eastern slope of Mount Moriah and into the gate of the city. There was dancing in the street. The crowds were singing at the top of their lungs as they waved their palm branches. A festive mood permeated the atmosphere. After all, everyone loves a parade.

But, in the midst of all the palm branches there were broken dreams. Most of the emphasis on Palm Sunday today is centered on the pep rally, the parade and the palm branches. But all that was really a sham. Our Lord knew this. In a few days they would all be gone and their cheers for Him would turn to jeers at Him.

Can you picture the Lord Jesus in this Palm Sunday scene? He is the center of attention. He must have had a smile on His face

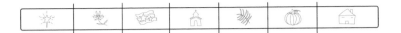

as He came riding down the hill on the back of that donkey as though He were in a convertible in a parade. The people were waving their palm branches, shouting and singing. The party was on. And then we read these words—"As He drew near, He saw the city and wept over it" *(Luke 19:41)*. Do you see Him? He is weeping! In the very midst of all the hoopla, He is weeping. Yes, there was a broken dream amid the palm branches.

His kingdom was not of this world. Over eighty times in the gospels He had spoken about "the Kingdom of God." But they didn't get it. They continued to raise their voices, shouting, "Blessed is the King who comes in the name of the Lord" *(Luke 19:38)*. They were not really celebrating because of Him but because of what they thought they could get from Him. They had missed it…and He knew it. Somehow they had read right past Isaiah's prophetic words of a coming suffering servant who would be wounded for our own transgressions.

Yes, they were cheering, all right. But He knew their hearts and thus the Bible records, "Now when He drew near, He saw the city and wept over it, saying, 'If you had known, even you, especially in this your day, the things that make for your peace! But now they are hidden from your eyes. For days will come upon you when your enemies will build an embankment around you, surround you and close you in on every side. And level you and your children within you, to the ground; and they will not leave in you one stone upon another, because you did not know the time of your visitation' " *(Luke 19:41-44)*. And so our Lord wept. He cried.

The crowds? They thought they were getting what they wanted. They thought they were welcoming a king who would deliver them from the oppression of Rome. They thought they were getting a liberator in the form of a "Stormin" Norman Schwarzkopf, or better yet, a Jewish George Washington who would liberate them against seemingly insurmountable odds. They only had eyes that day for their physical and temporal needs; not those needs that were spiritual and eternal.

When they realized they were not getting what they wanted a few days later, those Jerusalem crowds faded away and what was left were no longer cheering but jeering. Oh, we made Him a king, all right. We platted a crown of thorns and pressed it upon His brow and then mockingly bowed down with our sarcastic hails to the king. And we laughed. We beat Him. We spit on Him. We stripped Him naked and then we put a robe on Him, stuffed a reed for a scepter in His hand and mocked Him asking, "Are you the King of the Jews?" What a joke, we thought. And we laughed some more. He was a King, all right, but His kingdom was not of this world, it was a kingdom of the heart.

As our Lord rode down Palm Sunday Road that day, He knew how fickle the crowd really was and thus, He wept. He had come to really liberate them forever but they wanted no part of that. So in the midst of all the cheers...He cried. He knew. And so on Palm Sunday Road we find a broken dream in the midst of all the palm branches.

What do we do when our own dreams fall apart? How can we pick up the pieces of our broken dreams and begin to dream again? Our Lord is teaching us three things on this Palm Sunday. Broken dreams can hurt. He felt the pain of a broken dream and He wants us to know that when everyone else is waving their palms and shouting their hosannas that it is okay to cry. Broken dreams can hurt. He also wants to remind us that broken dreams can heal. He went from Palm Sunday to the Garden of Gethsemane where He prayed, "Not my will but Thine be done" *(Luke 22:42)*. Broken dreams can heal when God is in control. Finally, our Lord reminds us that broken dreams can help. He kept on doing right. He kept on moving forward on His journey to the cross with a renewed sense of dependence upon the Father. Let's look and learn as our Lord teaches us on this Palm Sunday about broken dreams and palm branches.

BROKEN DREAMS CAN HURT

"...and when He saw the city He wept over it." (Luke 19:41)

Look at our Lord. Can you picture the scene? He is seated on the back of a donkey and as He comes in view of the Holy City He begins to weep. This was not the first time we find Him shedding tears in scripture. Earlier, and ironically, on the same mountain although on the opposite slope, in the little village of Bethany, we read, "Jesus wept" *(John 11:35)*. He was standing at the tomb of His friend, Lazarus, and John records that He began to weep.

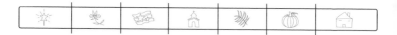

Interestingly, he uses the Greek word, δακρυω to describe this weeping. The word means to shed tears but in more of a silent vein. Thus, when He stood on the eastern slope of the Mount of Olives at Bethany, He did not weep with loud sobs, but more quietly. The word indicates that most likely a lump came in His throat; tears welled up in His eyes and spilled silently down His bronze cheeks.

But when we find Him weeping here on the western slope on Palm Sunday that particular word is not used to describe what was taking place. Here the word is indicating pain or deep grief which leads one to cry with deep and loud sobs. On that day you could have heard our Lord weeping two blocks away.

I have heard men and women who wept this way in pain. I have heard children weep this way when they are really hurt. A parent knows the difference in his or her child's cry when they are truly in pain. I have been with men and women who wept like this in grief as they stood at the open grave of a loved one. As a pastor I have heard the deep sobs of a mother whose only child met a tragic and sudden death. Incidentally, this same Greek word is used in Luke 22:62 when it tells us that Simon Peter, upon hearing the rooster crow, went out and "wept bitterly."

Look once more at the Lord Jesus. He is seated on the donkey. The people are cheering. The palm branches are waving. He tops the hill, sees the city, and begins to weep. Luke in writing this account is inspired to use this word that means to cry with loud and deep sobs. On Palm Sunday Road Jesus did not simply get a lump in His throat and brush a tear away before anyone saw it. No! He broke down and cried with loud sobs from a deeply grieved heart. Yes, broken dreams can hurt.

He had healed their sick. He had cleansed their lepers. He had fed their hungry. He had given hope to their depressed. But, He had failed to win their hearts. They wanted Him, all right, but primarily for what they could get from Him. So, the Lord Jesus, seated on a lowly donkey, broke into tears. This very One who had spoken the world into existence, flung the stars in place and put the planets in their orbits met the closed doors of the human hearts He had come to save. And it hurt.

Yes, broken dreams can hurt. Do you hear that...you with a broken dream? Look at Him. He cares. He says to any and all of us with broken dreams, "I understand. I have been there. I know." One of the lessons of Palm Sunday is that it is okay to cry. Broken dreams can hurt and it is no shame to acknowledge this fact.

When we see Him on this original Palm Sunday Road what does it say to us today? It reminds us that it is okay to cry. If we do not feel the hurt and grief of a broken dream, it was not much of a dream in the first place. God gives us the gift of tears in days of broken dreams and tears have a way of being therapeutic. The world tells us to be strong. The world tells us that others see our tears as a sign of weakness. But that is not the message of our Lord. He reminds us through Paul that we do not have to be strong. We can be weak because strength comes through weakness *(2 Corinthians 12:9-10).*

Some live with broken dreams on this Palm Sunday and they are too proud to admit it. So they ride down their own Palm Sunday Road with their shoulders tilted back, their heads held high and their jaws set like stone. And many of them live a

lifetime without real healing. In fact, those who insist on "staying strong" in the midst of broken dreams most usually become weak in the process. But the truth is…it is okay to cry. Jesus did.

What can be done about it? Be honest and stop trying to push your broken dreams into some imaginary closet. Admit it. Broken dreams can hurt. It is okay to cry. Some never learn to dream again for the simple fact that they allow their broken dreams to embitter them instead of allowing them to enable them to move on and dream again.

Broken dreams can hurt. But, only for a season. The Lord Jesus didn't cry forever. He went on from Palm Sunday to show us that broken dreams can also heal.

BROKEN DREAMS CAN HEAL

" 'Father, if it is Your will, take this cup away from me; nevertheless, not my will, but Yours, be done.' Then an angel appeared to Him from heaven strengthening Him." (Luke 22:42-43)

Look at our Lord now. He went from Palm Sunday to the Gethsemane Garden a few days later. He admitted His grief saying, "My soul is overwhelmed with sorrow" *(Matthew 26:38)*. But He left Gethsemane a victor. No more tears. No tears even in the face of His accusers, tormentors, persecutors and executioners. He was in charge! He had won the victory of Calvary in the garden the evening before. Hear Him— "Not my will but Yours be done." He found His comfort in the fact that the Father was in control of the situation. And the broken dreams of Palm Sunday found healing in the Garden of Gethsemane.

What does this say to us on our own Palm Sunday Roads this morning? Broken dreams can hurt. But, they can also heal when we come to the place of surrendering our will to His. One of the tragedies of modern Christianity is that we seem to have lost that word, "surrender." Perhaps in our western mindset we are just too macho. We would rather talk of conquest and commitment than to speak of surrender. But in the Christian life our Lord teaches us that surrender to His will is the only thing that brings true healing.

We all have our own share of broken dreams. The real issue becomes what we do with them. Some allow broken dreams to so embitter them that they live the rest of their lives with hurt. Others go on to a personal Gethsemane and allow them to heal. But the Lord Jesus teaches us there is more. Broken dreams can hurt. They can heal. And, broken dreams can also help.

B R O K E N   D R E A M S   C A N   H E L P

"...and He said, 'Peace to you.'...and He opened their understanding that they might comprehend the scriptures...and He led them out as far as Bethany, and He lifted up His hands and blessed them...and they worshipped Him, and returned to Jerusalem with great joy and were continually in the temple praising and blessing God." (Luke 24:36-53)

Yes, we can dream again! Our Lord kept doing what was right. Broken dreams that once hurt and then were healed now actually helped others along the way. The disciples had their own broken

dreams. On the Emmaus Road they lamented, "We had hoped He had been the one." Peter said he was going back to the fishing business. Scripture simply records, "They all forsook Him and fled." But, what a difference when they had been with Him. They "returned to Jerusalem with great joy." Broken dreams can help us face the future with courage.

Once the Lord left Gethsemane, the crowd's cheers on Palm Sunday turned to loud jeers before Pilate. But Jesus? He kept on walking toward the cross. He knew His best friends would desert Him, He would be humiliated, beaten and finally nailed to a cross but He never missed a step. He kept walking to Calvary. He faced it with courage. He died with dignity and a Roman soldier even exclaimed, "Surely, this was the Son of God."

What does all this say to us on this Palm Sunday? Be faithful where you are. God has a plan for you. Just because you have a broken dream, don't quit. Don't give up. Broken dreams can actually help you and bless others.

Many of those who have been most used of God seem to be those who have had their fair share of broken dreams and learned to dream again. They were those who got knocked down and then got back up. Simon Peter comes to mind. He followed from afar off after the arrest and found himself warming by a fire when Jesus was led by and simply "looked" at him. Peter learned that broken dreams can hurt. He went out and "wept bitterly" *(Luke 22:62)*. He also learned that broken dreams can heal. We find him a few days later seated at breakfast on the shore with the resurrected Christ affirming his love repeatedly. And, in Peter, we see that broken dreams can help. He went on

from there to become the undisputed leader of the Jerusalem church and the great preacher at Pentecost. Yes, broken dreams can end up helping.

We all start out with dreams. Many of them get broken along the way. Some of us are shouting our hosannas today, outwardly putting on a good front. But inwardly, we are filled with broken dreams. As we wave our palm branches today, does this story tell us anything about ourselves? Do we, like they, shout and support as long as we think we are going to get what we want? Do we shout our own hosannas because of who He is or because of what we want from Him? Even in the midst of our own Palm Sunday He may still be weeping. The good news on this Palm Sunday is that we can dream again.

After the Palm Sunday Parade whoever thought that in just a few days there would be a crucifixion? What a shock! But that is not the biggest shock. Whoever thought that after the crucifixion there would be a resurrection!

Where do we begin to dream again? We begin in the same place our Lord did. We begin in the same place Simon Peter did or anyone else who ever found healing. That is, at the feet of the Father in our own Gethsemane praying, "Not my will, but yours be done." Broken dreams can hurt. Broken dreams can heal. And broken dreams can help.

CHAPTER III.

EASTER SUNDAY

John 11:25-26

THERE ARE MANY QUESTIONS THAT FILL OUR MINDS DURING THE EASTER SEASON. What shall I wear? Did you order the lilies? Where will we hide the Easter eggs? Where will we eat Easter brunch and who should we invite? Should we attend the early worship service or the late? But there is one question that is truly Easter's bottom-line question. It is the question Jesus asked at Bethany when, after proclaiming that He, Himself, was the resurrection and the life and that those who believed and put their trust in Him would have eternal life, He asked, "Do you believe this?" *(John 11:26)*

The preacher's task on Easter morning is not to convince his hearers of the resurrection. After His resurrection He appeared to His disciples. They saw Him. They spoke with Him. But Thomas was absent and when told the good news he doubted and demanded proof for his own eyes. Quite frankly, if Simon Peter, James, John and the others could not convince Thomas, the preacher should be under no illusion that in a few minutes he is going to convince his own hearers. But, what he can do is confront each and every one of them with Easter's bottom-line question—"Do you believe this?"

The resurrection is what separates our Lord from a thousand other gurus and prophets who have come down the pike. Easter's bottom-line question drives any responsible hearer to either accept or reject the Christian faith. Almost yearly now there comes another book or movie, in the ilk of *The DaVinci Code,* that is nothing more than a blasphemous frontal attack on the claims of our Lord. This is nothing new. It is the same type Gnosticism the early church faced and the Apostle Paul confronted when he said, "Beware lest anyone deceive you through philosophy or empty deceit, according to the traditions of man, according to the basic principalities of the world and not according to Christ" *(Colossians 2:8).*

Our Easter text finds us this morning in Bethany. The Lord is standing at the tomb of His friend Lazarus and makes an astonishing claim, "I am the resurrection and the life. He who believes in Me, though he may die, he shall live. And whoever lives and believes in Me shall never die" *(John 11:25-26).* Then He looks into their faces, and into our hearts this morning and asks Easter's bottom-line question— "Do you believe this" *(John 11:26)?* Some try to avoid this question throughout life. Let it sink in a moment. "Do you believe this?"

In reading this text I have often wondered how our Lord inflected this question. Did He ask, "Do YOU believe this?" After all, it is personal. Did He ask, "Do you BELIEVE this?" It is, after all, pointed. Or, did he ask, "Do you believe THIS?" It is precise. May we on this Easter morning answer it in the fashion that it was answered in Bethany, "Yes, Lord, I believe

that You are the Christ, the Son of God, who is to come into the world" *(John 11:27).* Let's search Easter's bottom-line question for ourselves.

IT IS PERSONAL

"Do YOU believe this?" (John 11:26)

Perhaps the Lord put the inflection on the "you" in the question in order to drive home to our hearts that it is personal. After all, when it comes to saving faith in the finished work of Christ this is what matters most…not what my mother or my wife or anyone else believes. This is a personal matter. I have known people who have virtually lived their lives on what someone else believed as though they would eventually benefit by some sort of spiritual osmosis. Ultimately, Easter's bottom-line question is, "Do YOU believe this?"

An increasing number in our twenty-first century Gnostic culture are captivated by documentaries, movies and books which question the veracity of the gospel account. Is that what you really want to believe? That is, that Christ was really not the Son of God as He said He was? Do you want to believe that His death was an unnecessary event and not a voluntary, vicarious death for you? Or, that the account of the resurrection should be relegated to some ancient shelf of obscurity along with other myths and fables?

Easter's bottom-line question is personal. Jesus claimed to be "the resurrection and the life." Jesus is still asking today, "Do YOU believe this?"

IT IS POINTED

"Do you BELIEVE this?"

Perhaps when our Lord asked this question in Bethany He put added inflection and emphasis on the word "believe." After all, faith is the acceptable response to the Christian gospel. He was not inquiring of His hearers as to whether they were giving intellectual assent to His claims. But, He wanted to know if they would trust in Him and take Him at His word by faith. "Do you BELIEVE this?"

It is one thing to know about the gospel story intellectually. It is one thing to hear about it through one avenue or another. It is one thing to try to conform ourselves to it and to a new set of moral standards which accompany these truths. It is even one thing to argue for it apologetically and reason about it. It is, in fact, possible to conform to the truth of the gospel without ever being transformed from within by grace through faith.

The real issue on this Easter morning is, "Do you BELIEVE this?" Have you transferred your trust from yourself and your own good efforts over to Jesus Christ alone? Has this saving faith, this resurrected life, this "Christ in me" experience, made a difference in your life? Paul reminds us that it is "by grace

you have been saved by faith, and that not of yourselves; it is the gift of God, not of works, lest anyone should boast. For we are His workmanship, created in Christ Jesus for good works, which God prepared beforehand that we should walk in them" *(Ephesians 2:8-10).* Do you BELIEVE this?

IT IS PRECISE

"Do you believe THIS?"

Now we come to the heart of the issue, for true faith must rest on objective truth. It may be that the Lord Jesus inflected Easter's bottom-line question with His emphasis placed on the last word—"Do you believe THIS?"

"Do you believe THIS?" What we ask? THIS! What? Note the context. "I am the resurrection and the life. He who believes in me, though he may die, he shall live. And whoever lives and believes in me shall never die" *(John 11:25-26).* Immediately on the heels of this incredible attestation comes Easter's bottom-line question. "Do you believe THIS?"

HIS CLAIM ABOUT DEITY

"Do you believe THIS?"

"I am the resurrection and the life" *(John 11:25).* When He used that phrase, "I am," it captured the attention of those around

him. Seven times this "I am" affirmation is recorded in John's gospel. In John 6 Jesus said, "I am the bread of life." In John 8 He said, "I am the light of the world." In John 10 He said, "I am the door." In John 10 He also said, "I am the chief shepherd." In John 14 He proclaimed, "I am the way, the truth and the life." In John 15 we hear Him say, "I am the true vine." And here in our Easter text He states, "I am the resurrection and the life." He is the great "I am" and not the great "I was." We first hear God use this "I am" way back in Exodus 3:13-14. When Moses encountered the Living God in the burning bush he asked Him to reveal His name so that when he returned to Egypt with the message of emancipation, he might reveal who had sent him. God simply replied, "Tell him 'I AM' has sent you."

When our Lord made this statement at the tomb of Lazarus, all those around recognized it as an affirmation of deity. Modern day Gnostics tell us that Constantine muscled this truth of Christ's deity through the Nicene council in 325AD and into the Nicene Creed and that the church never believed it until then. If so, then why did John begin his gospel saying, "In the beginning was the Word and the Word was with God and the Word was God…and the Word became flesh and dwelt among us" *(John 1:1, 14)?*

The most fundamental belief of the Christian faith is that Jesus Christ is God Himself. This is why the Apostle Paul said, "He is the image of the invisible God…all things were created by Him and for Him" *(Colossians 1:15-16).* It was this faith in the deity of Christ that led all the apostles except John to their own martyr's deaths. It was the insistence upon this Christological truth that

had Ignatius of Antioch thrown to the wild animals at the end of the first century and Polycarp of Smyrna burned at the stake a few decades later. Easter's bottom-line question is precise— "Do you believe THIS?"

Martha answered this question immediately, "Yes, Lord, I believe that You are the Christ, the Son of God, who is to come into the world" *(John 11:27)*. Martha was a devout Jew. When she used the word "Christ," χριστος, it had a deep meaning to all those who heard this confession. Their minds went immediately to the Temple and the Passover season when the sacrificial lambs were slain and when the High Priest on the Day of Atonement, Yom Kippur, entered the Holy of Holies to sprinkle the blood over the Mercy Seat above the Ark of the Covenant. Yom Kippur means "day of covering." It was then that the sins of the people were "covered" by the blood. Like most people today I use a credit card. When I go to make a purchase, I give them my card and they accept it as cash. Now, that plastic card has no real intrinsic value in or of itself. But it is accepted. Why? It is a forerunner of the true cash payment that soon will come when I receive my monthly bill. Until then the credit card "covers" my purchase. As such the Old Covenant "covered" the sins of the people who looked for Christos, the Anointed One, the Christ who was to come to make final payment for the sins of the world. And He did and it is no wonder there have not been sacrifices made on Temple Mount in 2,000 years now. All that was in Martha's reply. "Yes, Lord, I believe that You are the Christ."

Who is He to you this Easter season? Merely some figure out of history? Or, the subject of some sentimental story out of childhood? Or, can you say with Martha, "Yes, Lord, I believe that You are the Christ." Easter's bottom-line question is precise. "Do you believe THIS?" That is, His claim about deity?

HIS CLAIM ABOUT DEATH

"Do you believe THIS?"—"though he may die" *(John 11:25)*. Many live their lives in total denial of their coming appointment with death. Jesus says that one of the facts of life is that we are going to die. Do you believe THIS?

Recently I was going through a stack of pictures that were made a decade ago. I was stunned. My hair was darker then. I certainly looked younger in the face. It dawned on me that this body of mine has death in it. I am decaying before my eyes. Certain parts of me are seeing some deterioration. Oh, some opt for plastic surgery. Others for liposuction. Others eat vitamin-enriched foods and do all they can to keep their cholesterol down. But none of us can stop the fact that we are marching toward the grave. Death is our final enemy.

Death is the real common denominator of all men. If you do not believe it, just pick up the obituary section in any city newspaper. On the society page you will read about only one class of people. In the business section you will read about those who are excelling in various professions. In the sports section you will read about those who are athletically gifted. But on the

obituary page everyone is listed side by side and usually in a cold alphabetical order. The rich and the poor side by side. The talented and the not so gifted side by side. The famous and the not so famous side by side. Death knocks on the door of the wealthiest billionaire and the poorest peasant and sends them both to stand before the Judge of all the earth. Yes, death is man's common denominator.

There are a lot of books on the best-seller lists that tell us how to live today. But there is only one Book that tells us how to die. Easter's bottom-line question is not just personal and pointed, it is precise—"Do you believe THIS?" Do you believe our Lord's claim about death?

Long centuries ago the prophet Amos thundered down his warning, "Prepare to meet your God" *(Amos 4:12)*. We prepare for everything in life. Your medical doctor didn't just hang out a shingle that announced his or her medical practice. Years of study, preparation and planning went into that. We prepare for everything in life. We prepare for our children's college education. We even prepare for those we will leave behind through various insurance policies and the like. But too few of us "prepare to meet our God." The Bible says, "It is appointed unto man once to die and after this the judgment" *(Hebrews 9:27)*. Isn't it foolish to spend all our time and energies on this life alone when there is another life that is more than a million times a million times longer than this one? Every one of us has an appointment with death. "Do you believe THIS?" That is His claim about death.

H I S   C L A I M   A B O U T   D E S T I N Y

"Do you believe THIS?"—"he shall live" *(John 11:25)*. It is strange how so many today live their lives as if this were all there is. Jesus indicates here that even though death is sure, we are going to live again. The body may indeed die, but not the Spirit, not that part of you that will live as long as God lives and then one day be reunited with a glorified body for the endless ages of eternity. Do you believe His claim that even though we may die we will, in fact, live again?

At this writing one of our daughters is pregnant with our fifth grandchild. Watching that little package of love grow inside her all these months has been beautiful. I once heard of a hypothetical conversation between a mother and her unborn child. "In just a few days you are going to be born," excitedly declares the mom. "But I don't want to be born. I don't want to leave this womb. I like it here. It is comfortable and warm. I feel so secure and cozy here. I like it like this," argues the soon-to-be-born baby. The mom continues, "But, you don't realize what you are missing. There is laughter and sunshine and there are brothers and sisters with whom to play. And, there is music and picnics and toys." And the debate continues with the baby arguing against the very idea of birth because she cannot begin to relate experientially to the concept. The baby does not understand that to remain in the womb too long could result in tragic consequences.

Some of us today struggle against the thought of death in the same way and with the same ignorance. Why? Because we do not understand Easter's bottom-line question with

its accompanying fact that, "though we shall die, we shall live again."

The real question for many of us on this Easter morning is, "What are we doing about that part of us that is going to live forever?" Many do not want to think about this on an Easter morning. After all, we have new dresses and shoes and a big family lunch on the day's agenda. And sadly, fewer churches in the western world ever confront their hearers with Easter's bottom-line question anymore due to this "feel good" culture which permeates most every part of our being. But Easter confronts us with a question for eternity—"Do you believe THIS?" What? His claim about deity, "I am the Resurrection and the Life." His claim about death, "he who believes in Me though he dies." His claim about destiny, "he shall live."

HIS CLAIM ABOUT DELIVERANCE

"Do you believe THIS?"—"whoever lives and believes in Me shall never die" *(John 11:26)*. The Lord is making it very plain here. Eternal salvation is through faith in Him alone and not through human effort or good works. And note, "whoever LIVES and believes in Me shall never die." Faith is only possible this side of the grave. In the Sermon on the Mount, Jesus spoke of those who would make their appeal after this life to whom he will reply, "I never knew you" *(Matthew 7:23)*. Eternal life can be ours in this life now and through faith in Him alone. It is no wonder Paul said, "In Him we have redemption through

His blood, the forgiveness of sins, according to the riches of His grace" *(Ephesians 1:7).*

Easter is a day of decision when we are confronted with its bottom-line question. In fact, there are only three possible responses to His Easter claims. One, He was divine. And thus, He did in fact rise from the dead. His body was gone. His friends surely did not take it. They had already fled in fear and cowardice. His foes did not have the body. They would have loved to present His dead body before those who were later heralding His resurrection. Another possibility is that He was deceptive. That is, that Jesus was a sort of con artist as portrayed in some modern movies and blasphemous books. Was He simply deceiving people by claiming to be "the Resurrection and the Life?" The only other possibility was that He was demented, some kind of a first century David Koresh.

On this Easter morning if you do not believe He was demented or deceived, then you must believe He was divine, who He said He was! The Lord! If so, then what do you intend to do about it? Will you simply continue to tip your hat to Him at Christmas and Easter or will you face Easter's bottom-line question? "Do you believe this?" Do you believe that He is Lord, that you will one day die, that you will live again, and that if you put your trust and faith in Him alone you will inherit eternal life?

There are a lot of big questions in life. Where will I attend college? What vocation shall I pursue? Whom shall I marry? But there is only one big question in death. "Do you believe this?" That's it. "Do you believe this?" It is personal. "Do YOU believe this?" You cannot live your life on what someone else believes.

It is pointed. "Do you BELIEVE this?" Faith is the key. It is precise. "Do you believe THIS?" Jesus Christ is Lord and if you put your faith in Him alone to save you, you will never die.

Look at Lazarus in the context of our question. He is a picture of all of us. He is dead. There is nothing he can do for himself to bring life. But then Christ calls for him and brings him out of death and into life *(John 11:43-44)*. This same Jesus calls us out of spiritual death and darkness into a brand new life with Him.

Finally, note Martha's own reply to Easter's bottom-line question—"Yes, Lord, I believe that You are the Christ, the Son of God, who is to come into the world" *(John 11:27)*. Would you join her on this Easter morning by simply saying, "Yes, Lord, I believe"?

CHAPTER IV.

COMMUNION SUNDAY

1 Corinthians 11:23-28

"FOR I RECEIVED FROM THE LORD THAT WHICH I ALSO DELIVERED TO YOU; THAT THE LORD JESUS ON THE SAME NIGHT IN WHICH HE WAS BETRAYED TOOK BREAD; AND WHEN HE HAD GIVEN THANKS, HE BROKE IT..." *(1 Corinthians 11:23-24).* And so, with these old and often repeated words Paul begins his instruction pertaining to the receiving of the bread and the cup of the Lord's Supper.

It was the evening before His crucifixion, "the night in which He was betrayed," that the Lord arranged to borrow an upper room on Mount Zion to host His disciples for the Jewish Seder meal at which He instituted a new supper to be done "in remembrance of Me." We call this memorial meal the "Lord's Supper." And, rightly so. It is His and not ours. He does the inviting. Whenever we partake in this act of remembrance we are invited guests, as were the disciples in the upper room that fateful evening.

Why have we Christians been gathering in churches, in homes, in catacombs, in hidden basements, in prison cells and a myriad of other places down through the centuries to observe this meal? We do so in order that we might grant His request to "do this in remembrance of Me" *(1 Corinthians 11:24).* In the language of

the New Testament the word here means to call back into our memories a vivid experience from the past and meditate upon it. The Greek text denotes indefinite repetition, that is, to do it again and again and again.

Our family has a large family photo album which virtually tells the story of each of our lives from birth until now. If you were to sit on our sofa and thumb through it, it would, most likely, not mean much to you. You would see my old home place on Crenshaw Street in Fort Worth. It is a little two bedroom, one bath, frame home with a white picket fence and a mimosa tree out in front. You would then quickly turn the page having seen it. But, when I see it, memories abound of experiences in that old house. When I look at that picture it reminds me of a scar I still carry on my leg where I fell on that fence trying to climb over it one day. My dad had told me a thousand times to stay off it but I thought I knew best.

Susie's and my first home is in that family picture album. That tiny little three-room house behind another house would mean nothing to you. But when I look at it, it brings up memories of joy and happiness of those first few months of marriage. Just looking at it reminds me of how ice would build up on the inside of our windows at night since the entire place was heated with only one small portable electric floor heater which would be moved from room to room. Warm and wonderful are fond family memories.

In the same way in which my family photo album brings to mind so many memories of bygone days, so do the bread and the cup of the Lord's Supper table for members of God's family. It may not mean much to those who have not been born into

His family; but for those of us who have, it stirs in our hearts thankful memories of His sacrifice for us. This is one of the reasons that the Lord's Supper is only for those who have, by faith, been born again into the family of God.

Paul says that by partaking of this supper we "proclaim the Lord's death" *(1 Corinthians 11:26)*. He uses the Greek word, καταγγελλω, here which means that we are preaching a sermon, proclaiming a message, when we come to the Lord's Table. You say, "I could never preach a sermon." But you do, each time you take of the cup and the bread. You are retelling the story of the cross and His vicarious death for us. The Lord's Supper and baptism are sermons we all preach about the substitutionary, vicarious death of the Lord Jesus Christ. After all, the best of all the sermons are the ones preached by our lives and not simply our lips.

So as we come to the Lord's Supper we are preaching a sermon. Our sermon has four points. There is a word of explanation, a word of exaltation, a word of expectation and a word of examination.

A   W O R D   O F   E X P L A N A T I O N

"For I received from the Lord that which I also delivered to you; that the Lord Jesus on the same night in which He was betrayed took bread…" (1 Corinthians 11:23)

Initially, there is a word of explanation about that "which has been delivered" to us. The Lord's Supper is an ordinance of

Christ given to His church. An ordinance is a ceremony the Lord Jesus commanded His church to observe in this dispensation of grace which tells the story of the gospel in a symbolic or metaphorical form. There are two such ordinances of the church. One is baptism. In this act of obedience following our conversion experience the death, burial and resurrection of our Lord is beautifully pictured in our baptism by immersion. While this act does nothing to save us or wash away our sins, it is one of the first steps of obedience for every believer. The other ordinance given us by our Lord is the Lord's Supper. While there is no saving grace in the digesting of the elements, it does show forth a beautiful picture of our Lord's broken body in the unleavened bread and His shed blood in the cup.

The Lord's Supper is not a ritual that is to be repeatedly observed in such a fashion that it loses its significance. Our Roman Catholic friends believe in what is termed transubstantiation. This belief holds to the fact that quite literally and actually the elements of the bread and the cup become the body and blood of the Lord. However, on that night when it was instituted, He said, "This is my body…," and the reality was they still enjoyed his actual physical presence in his real body at that moment. Our Lutheran friends hold to a belief called consubstantiation. This teaches that while the elements are still in fact bread and the fruit of the vine some mystical transformation ensues as they are taken into our bodies.

We, who are called Baptists, believe that the elements are symbolic. That is, that the bread and the cup are simply "pictures"

of His broken body and shed blood. Scriptural interpretation comes in many forms. Sometimes Jesus spoke in parables, stories that told eternal truths. Who of us could ever forget the parable of the Prodigal Son? On other occasions Jesus spoke with simile. For example, the Bible speaks of the Spirit descending "like a dove" at His baptism. He also spoke in hyperbole, exaggerated expressions to drive home simple truths. Once, He said if our eye was offending us to "pluck it out." That is an obvious hyperbole, especially when interpreted in light of all other scripture. And, often our Lord spoke metaphorically. He said in the Sermon on the Mount that His followers were to be "the salt of the earth." He did not mean that we were literally to be salt but that we were to season life with His goodness and preserve our culture from decay. And thus, in the same manner, the elements of the Lord's Supper are metaphorical expressions of His body and blood.

One of the most misunderstood and confusing portions of this text is in Paul's statement that, "Whoever eats this bread or drinks this cup of the Lord in an unworthy manner will be guilty of the body and blood of the Lord" *(1 Corinthians 11:27)*. Some who read these words inserted in this beautiful and instructive passage feel they are unworthy to come to the Lord's Table. If the receiving of these elements depended upon our own worthiness, who of us could approach the table? The adverb used here in verse 27 means of "unequal weight." The word picture is of a scale tipping down on one side with one side heavier than the other. On either side of that scale are our heart and our conduct, our faith and our works. This is not a question of worth or worthiness. After all,

Paul called himself "less than the least of all the saints" in the Ephesian letter and in his last epistle to Timothy he referred to himself as "the chief of sinners." This verse speaks of an attempt by the unconverted, the unrepentant and the unreconciled to come to the Lord's Table. It involves a cavalier approach.

There is a word of explanation. The Lord's Supper is a picture of the broken body and shed blood of our Lord in our behalf. There is no saving grace in the actual partaking of it but it is a "sermon" each of us preaches about His atoning sacrifice for our sins and a remembrance of Him.

A WORD OF EXALTATION

"And when He had given thanks He broke it…."
(1 Corinthians 11:24)

The second point in the sermon we preach at the Lord's Table is a word of exaltation. How we exalt Him today for His broken body and shed blood that made a way out of no way for us. Note, when He "had given thanks He broke it." He broke it. How prophetic. The cross was no accident. He willingly, voluntarily, laid down His life. In John 10:18 we hear Him proclaim, "No one takes it (my life) from Me for I lay it down Myself."

The Lord's Supper is a time of thanksgiving. The very word "Eucharist" comes from this Greek expression in verse 24 of giving thanks. We are a thankful people. In the

busyness of our lives we are so prone to be forgetful. We tend to forget names and promises and even the purpose of our Lord's coming. And so He brings us to His table and says, "This do in remembrance of Me" *(1 Corinthians 11:25).*

He died...for me! The Lord Jesus gave Himself for me... and you. He didn't die in a white starched shirt with an expensive tie on some gold cross on a mahogany communion table in a high-steeple, stained-glass church. But out there where people were shouting and cursing and sweating. It was there that "He who knew no sin became sin for me that I might become the righteousness of God in Him" *(2 Corinthians 5:21).*

We do not partake of the Lord's Supper to remind Him; but to remember Him. In remembering His death for us we exalt Him and give Him praise and thanks. We are a thankful people.

A W O R D O F E X P E C T A T I O N

"...you proclaim the Lord's death till He comes."
(1 Corinthians 11:26)

The Lord's Supper experience is not simply an acknowledgment of His physical absence but a promise of His physical return. There was a word that was constantly escaping the lips of those first generational believers. "Maranatha!" The Lord is coming. They greeted each other with that word. They comforted one

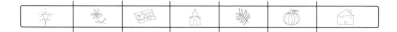

another with that word. They shouted it to one another in the final moments of martyrdom. They lived with the hope of His soon coming. When we partake of this memorial supper, we join them in proclaiming the Lord's vicarious death "until He comes" again.

When He comes again, we will never again take the Lord's Supper in the way we do today. It is only given to the church in this dispensation of grace. Why? There will be no need for it. We will have Him who the Supper pictures.

When I travel, I have had a habit of taking my wife's picture along with me. I like to place it by the phone on the nightstand of the hotel room as a reminder of how much I love and miss her. But, I don't do that when I get home. I have her actual presence which is so much more meaningful than a picture.

One golden daybreak our Lord is coming back to take us home. Now, while we are separated from His visible presence we put His picture out at the Lord's Supper table. But there is coming a day when He will seat us at His table and what a day that will be! But until then, we eat of the bread and drink of the cup to "proclaim the Lord's death till He comes." There is not simply a word of explanation, a word of exaltation and a word of expectation. Finally, there is a word of examination.

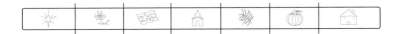

A WORD OF EXAMINATION

"But let a man examine himself and so let him eat of the bread and drink of the cup." (1 Corinthians 11:28)

The Lord's Table should be a time of self-examination. The Greek word here translated, "examine," is δοκιμαζω. It literally is saying, "Let a man put himself on trial. Let a man search his own heart; shining a light into its hidden recesses to see if there is any wicked thing revealed." Here is the necessary factor of confession of sin.

Note the admonition to examine ourselves before we "eat of the bread and drink of the cup." Here, we search our hearts for sins of the tongue; things we might have said which shouldn't have been voiced. Here, we search our hearts for sins of action; things we may have done that should not have been acted out. Here, we search our hearts for sins of thought; things we have harbored in our minds. Our mind is like a hotel. The manager of the hotel cannot keep someone from entering the lobby but he can keep him from getting a room. It is not a sin for something to pass through our minds. The problem comes when we give it a room. Here, we also search our hearts for sins of omission, things we should have done that were left undone. Once this search is complete we "confess our sins" knowing that "He is faithful and just to forgive our sins and to cleanse us from all unrighteousness" *(1 John 1:9)*.

Thus, at the Lord's Supper table we look backward with a word of explanation. We look upward with a word of exaltation.

We look forward with a word of expectation. And, we look inward with a word of examination.

Interestingly, there are usually six words written on every communion table in the world—"This do in remembrance of me." In the first century world when this admonition was given there were no cameras, no videos, no mobile phones with built-in cameras. No one ever took a picture of Jesus. Some seem to think that in daVinci's famous depiction of the Lord's Supper that some photographer said, "Okay, everyone please get on one side of the table for the picture." No. Jesus simply said, "This do in remembrance of Me…eat this bread and drink this cup."

Leonardo daVinci was commissioned by the Duke of Milan to paint the famous masterpiece we now know as the Last Supper. He labored over it for several years giving precise attention to every minute detail including that of the disciples' faces. He painted the table, the grouping, the chalice and finally the face of our Lord. When the work was completed, he showed it to a close confidant. He was awestruck by this marvelous work and said, "Oh, what a beautiful chalice. I cannot take my eyes off it." daVinci immediately took his brush and painted through the chalice so that nothing would ever take precedence over the face of Christ. And so it should be for us when we come to the Lord's Table. His presence with us should reign supreme.

The Lord's Supper is our own photo album, as it were, where we can come and remember what He has done for us. For me it calls to memory that cold January morning when as a seventeen-year-old young man "old things passed away and all became new" when I put my trust in Him. As often as we eat of the

bread and drink of the cup "we do show the Lord's death until He comes." Maranatha!

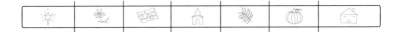

CHAPTER V.

M O T H E R ' S   D A Y

Matthew 1:5

IT IS MOTHER'S DAY AND ALL OVER THE CHRISTIAN
WORLD PREACHERS ARE POINTING THIS MORNING TO
THE MOTHER WE HAVE COME TO CALL THE "PROVERBS
31 WOMAN." What a lady. This wonder woman gets up before
dawn and stays busy until the early hours of the next morning.
We have developed a mental image of her. She has the looks of
a movie star, the domestic abilities of a master chef, the stamina
of a world-class athlete, the intellect of a professor with a PhD,
the tenacity of a political operative, the wisdom of a godly
missionary, the sensitivity of a Mother Teresa, the business sense
of a Fortune 500 executive, the grace of an etiquette expert and
the spirituality of the Virgin Mary. Wow. No wonder so many
mothers leave church feeling down on Mother's Day!

Can any of us measure up to this standard of perfection? She
is certainly a worthy goal for which to aim but we are all in
a process here. If it is the church's intent to reach her city for
Christ, then she must begin to deal with men and women where
they are and not simply where each of us should be.

In preparation for this Mother's Day message, I asked myself a question, "If the Lord Jesus was in my pulpit Sunday and preaching audibly what would He say?" I am convinced He wouldn't simply speak trite platitudes or read a sweet poem or two. I believe He would do exactly what He did in scripture. He would leave the ninety and nine and go after that one who is hurting and lost. Perhaps, it is the woman today who has never borne children. Or, the one who aborted her child in the past. Or, the mother who birthed a child and loved him so much that she entrusted him to someone else to raise and wonders, today, what he looks like and where he lives. On this Mother's Day let's allow our Lord to speak to each of us at the very point of our need.

While the woman in Proverbs 31 is a worthy example to emulate, she is not among those listed in the lineage of our Lord. But two women in Matthew 1:5 are listed there for all posterity to see. Who are these two mothers? They must be paragons of faithfulness to be in this righteous list. Not really. One is Rahab, the prostitute of Jericho. She was the madam who ran the house of ill repute in that ancient town in the Jordan valley. The other mother listed is Ruth, the godless Moabite. She was raised in a heathen environment worshipping pagan idols and gods. But something wonderful happened to each of these two mothers. Their experience with the living God caused them to be converted into two of the godliest mothers in the Bible and they live on in history and in heaven today.

Rahab and Ruth were mothers who overcame their circumstances. Like many modern moms they were torn between work and childcare. Many moms are divorced today; others may

be remarried and they are dealing with incredible adjustments and the struggle of divided loyalties. Others live with all sorts of unspoken heartaches in the home and are making the best of very difficult situations. Still others have husbands who cannot be trusted.

Rahab is listed here in the genealogy of Jesus to show us that there is hope for those who have been engaged in sinful pleasures. Ruth joins her in this list to show us that there is hope for those who have been engaged with societal pressures. Both of these women are remembered forever as virtuous women. Let's look at them and learn from them on this Mother's Day.

RAHAB SHOWS US WE CAN OVERCOME SINFUL PLEASURES

Who is this mother, named Rahab, listed here in Matthew 1 in the genealogy of Jesus? Her story is told in the second and sixth chapters of the book of Joshua. Here we find a lady with a reputation that was far from spotless. She was quite popular with the men who stopped in their caravans while journeying through the oasis city of Jericho. Everyone knew where her house was located. The local kids would point to it as they passed by. Five of the six times she is mentioned in scripture the word, "harlot," is placed alongside her name as if it were glued to her. When her family members are listed in Joshua 2:13, there is no mention of a husband or children. She was a lady who was involved in sinful pleasures.

When the Israelites sent spies into her city as they were about to begin their conquest of Canaan, she took them in. Interestingly, she had not heard what they had done for God during their march to the Promised Land, nor how well trained their armies had become, but what struck this harlot's heart was what the Living God had done for them and through them *(Joshua 2:10)*.

She becomes a beautiful example of how one can overcome her sinful pleasures to become a godly mother. Listen to her testimony in front of the Israelite spies, "I know that the Lord has given you the land, that the terror of you has fallen on us and that all the inhabitants of the land are fainthearted because of you. For we have heard how the Lord dried up the water of the Red Sea for you when you came out of Egypt, and what you did to the two kings of the Amorites who were on the other side of the Jordan, Sihon and Og, whom you utterly destroyed. And as soon as we heard these things our hearts melted; neither did there remain any courage in anyone because of you, for the Lord your God, He is God in heaven above and on earth beneath" *(Joshua 2:9-11)*. Here are the words spoken by one with a repentant heart—"He is God in heaven above and on earth beneath."

There is an interesting insight found a few verses earlier. She took the spies up on her roof and hid them under "the stalks of flax which she had laid in order on the roof" *(Joshua 2:6)*. Why was there flax on this woman's roof, neatly and orderly laid out? In the ancient world flax was gathered by industrious women, dried out and used for spinning and weaving. The presence of such a large quantity of it on her roof may well indicate she had experienced a change of

vocation. Interestingly enough, it is said of the Proverbs 31 woman that "she seeks wool and flax and works willingly with her hands" *(Proverbs 31:13).*

Not only did this woman of Jericho repent, but there is good evidence that she placed her faith in the living God *(Joshua 2:15-21).* When the spies went on their way with a promise to return, they told her to hang a scarlet thread out the window of her home so that when they came to conquer the city, her home would be spared. She replied, "According to your words, so be it. And she sent them away...and she bound the scarlet cord in the window" *(Joshua 2:21).*

When Rahab said "Yes," to the God of heaven and by faith hung the scarlet cord out her window, an amazing thing happened. God in heaven knew about a coming cross of which she was unaware. The blood was shed on that cross before the foundation of the world. God saw that cross and the salvation it so freely offered and looked down on her faith and saved her by His own blood. And, as a celebration of her faith, she hung that scarlet thread out her window, so that when judgment came and the walls came tumbling down, there was one obvious part of that wall that judgment could not touch because of the scarlet thread. Here is a beautiful picture of salvation tucked away in the Old Testament.

Rahab is listed in the lineage of Jesus in Matthew 1:5 to show all posterity that there is hope for any and all who trust in the living God.

What ever happened to her? Did she ever find a husband? I'll say she did. She lived among the Israelites and fell in love with

a prince by the name of Salmon. God blessed their union with a son whose name was Boaz, who became the Kinsman-Redeemer. This former harlot of Jericho became the mother of Boaz, the Lord of the harvest, who became the husband of Ruth.

Look at Rahab. She is remembered today on this Mother's Day to remind us there is hope for those who may have once lived in sinful pleasures of various types. And today, she lives on in history and in heaven as a good and godly mother who imparted the same qualities to her own family.

RUTH SHOWS US WE CAN OVERCOME SOCIETAL PRESSURES

Who is this other mother listed in Matthew 1:5 in the lineage of Jesus? Her name is Ruth. She was a Moabitess. Her obstacle was not that of sinful pleasures but of societal pressures. She was raised in a godless home, not unlike many in the western world today. She was raised in a pagan, anti-God culture. All the influences of her childhood were against her coming to know the living Lord.

She was a member of a race that actually began in incest *(Genesis 19:30-37)*. Lot slept with his own daughter and she bore a son named Moab. The Moabites did not worship the Lord God. They worshipped the pagan god, Chemosh. They offered human sacrifices to him. They were a degenerate people who resorted to all types of licentious behavior.

As a pastor for decades I have noticed that of all the strongholds, the religion of our childhood is the most difficult to break. It seems to have a hold over people. While Satan comes against those in sinful pleasure with accusations, he comes against those with societal pressures with obligations. Ruth is listed here in Matthew 1:5 as a godly mother to show us all that there is hope for those with societal pressures and a sense of false obligations to the religion of childhood.

How did Ruth become an overcomer? She saw her mother-in-law, Naomi, repent and set her face back to Bethlehem and away from Moab. Ruth began to cling to her with these words, "Entreat me not to leave you, or to turn back from following after you; for wherever you go, I will go; and wherever you lodge, I will lodge; your people shall be my people, and your God, my God; where you die, I will die, and there will I be buried" *(Ruth 1:16-17).* If you want to witness an Old Testament conversion, there it is.

Ruth found a *new determination.* "Entreat me not to leave you." All influences were against her. The religion of her childhood was against her. Orpah's example (she kissed Naomi and "went back to her people and her gods"), was against her. Naomi's insistence that she stay in Moab was against her. But faith brought a new determination in Ruth.

Ruth found a *new direction.* "Wherever you go, I will go." Ruth was determined that following the God of Naomi would become her new life's direction.

Ruth found a *new dependence.* "Wherever you lodge, I will lodge." She was saying that she would trust the Lord and Naomi for her basic needs.

Ruth found a *new desire.* "Your people shall be my people." Ruth knew that if she took the God of the Bible to be her God, then she would take His people as hers also. It did not take me long as a new believer to understand that if I was truly going to go God's way, then I had to do so in the company of His people.

Ruth found a *new devotion.* "Your God shall be my God." The interesting thing about this to me is that all she knew of Naomi's God was a God of suffering and sorrow. Naomi's husband had died, her two sons had died and her heart was filled with grief. But Ruth watched Naomi and knew her and her living testimony brought a new devotion to Ruth.

Ruth found a *new dedication.* "Wherever you die, I will die." Ruth was saying, "This is for life. This is a life decision. I am not coming back if things do not work out just the way I think they should."

Finally, Ruth found a *new destiny.* "Where you are buried I will be buried." I believe Ruth was saying here that "not even death will separate us."

What happened to this formerly godless Moabite woman? Did she find a husband? I'll say she did. Did she become a godly mother? Did she ever! Matthew 1:5 tells us the story. She returned to Bethlehem with Naomi. She married Boaz, the Lord of the harvest. You remember Boaz. He was the son of Rahab. Boaz and Ruth had a son whose name was Obed who had a son whose name was Jesse who had a son whose name was David. Yes, King David, the shepherd, the Psalmist, the king. I am sure this trust in the Living God was transferred to her great

grandson for later he would write, "I have been young and now I am old, but I have never seen the righteous forsaken nor his seed begging bread" *(Psalm 37:25).*

No more fitting tribute has ever been paid to a wife than when Ruth's husband said, "All the people of my town know that you are a virtuous woman" *(Ruth 3:11).* Look at Ruth. She stands there in the lineage of Jesus to show us that no matter what our past we can become virtuous through the Lord Jesus Christ.

Yes, if our Lord were here this Mother's Day physically and speaking audibly to us, I have no doubt he would leave the ninety and nine and come to each troubled, lonely or lost heart in order to impart and impute His righteousness to all who would believe so that it might be repeated that "all the people of our town might know that you are a virtuous woman."

It was not common in the ancient world to list women in a genealogy tree. In fact, in the entire listing of those in the line of Jesus which consumes most of the initial chapter of the New Testament only four women are mentioned. One might think they must have been some kind of virtuous women. But a closer look reveals an interesting truth. One is Tamar. She dressed as a prostitute, seduced her own father-in-law and had an illegitimate baby. The next is Rahab, the harlot, followed by Ruth, the Moabitess. Finally, we meet Bathsheba. She is the one who lived in adultery with King David. What do you suppose our Lord is trying to tell us on this Mother's Day? I think He is reminding us all that "if anyone be in Christ, he is a new creation, old things are passed away, and all becomes new"*(2 Corinthians 5:17).* The

gospel of the Lord Jesus Christ is the Good News of hope for any and all on this special day.

CHAPTER VI.

M E M O R I A L   D A Y

Daniel 5:1-31

MEMORIAL DAY IS UNIQUELY AN AMERICAN EXPERIENCE. We pause on this day each year to remember those who expressed what our Lord referred to as "greater love" who "laid down their lives" for family, friends and freedom. One week after the Pearl Harbor attack then President Franklin D. Roosevelt said, "Those who long enjoy such privileges that we enjoy forget in time that others have died to win them." Freedom is never really free; it is most always bought with the blood of patriots.

The biggest battle Americans are waging today is a battle for the very soul of a nation. We see it manifested in a myriad of ways every day. The erosion of a culture is a slow process but we have seen it accelerate rapidly in the past few short years. In the broader picture it continues to erode whether there is a Democrat or a Republican sitting in the Oval Office. We have today what we tolerated yesterday. And, we will inherit tomorrow what we tolerate today.

History has its own way of repeating itself down through the centuries. In his day, in the midst of a Babylonian culture, Daniel saw much of what we seem to be seeing today. Yet, his situation

was even worse. We read in the fifth chapter of Daniel of the collapse of a culture. They had felt so smug and secure within the confines of their strong walls. But, they crumbled from within. Babylon made four major mistakes. They lost all sense of remembrance. They lost all sense of reality. They lost all sense of restraint. And, they lost all sense of respect. On this Memorial Day may we be challenged to call our people to repentance and to acknowledge that "all is vain unless the Spirit" comes down upon us.

THE DANGER OF LOSING ALL SENSE OF REMEMBRANCE

"...the Most High God rules in the kingdom of men...but you have lifted yourself up against the Lord of Heaven..."
(Daniel 5:18-23)

Belshazzar's problem was the same as many today. This King of Babylon had forgotten some of the valuable lessons from the past. He had forgotten lessons like his predecessor, Nebuchadnezzar, had learned the hard way. Lessons like, "Those who walk in pride He is able to put down" *(Daniel 4:37).*

Pride is most often the predecessor to destruction. Daniel gives us a pertinent insight when he challenges the king with the accusation that "you have lifted yourself up against the Lord of Heaven." To "lift one's self up" means to boast, to elevate, and to lift up. This is exactly what Belshazzar had been doing, that is, boasting about himself. He picked up right where King

Nebuchadnezzar left off, saying, "Is not this great Babylon, that I have built for a royal dwelling by my mighty power and for the honor of my majesty *(Daniel 4:30)?"*

Pride always leads to a fall. It is right up there at the top of the list of those things which God hates. Just ask Lucifer about this. Ask Adam and Eve. Ask King David. Ask Simon Peter. Yes, "Those who walk in pride He is able to put down" *(Daniel 4:37).*

Our own nation once honored God unashamedly and openly. The truth of this is etched in numerous marble monuments all over the nation's capital. It is carved in granite on many of the government buildings we hold dear. It is printed on our currency. We once credited Him with our blessings and our successes and turned to Him in our trials and our losses. But today, we, like Babylon, seem to have lost a sense of remembrance. President Woodrow Wilson said, "A nation that does not remember what it was yesterday does not know what it is today, or what it is trying to do. We are about a futile thing if we do not know where we came from or what we have been about."

In some ways we have forgotten our past. What was it about America that made her so great and caused men and women from the nations of the world to risk their lives and fortunes to make her their home? Is there something about America that distinguishes us from our neighbors to the north and south? Canada was settled by French explorers who were looking for gold. Mexico was settled by Spanish explorers who were also looking for gold. America was settled by men and women who came here primarily looking for God. They came searching for a home where the Lord Jesus could be exalted and worshiped in spirit, freedom and truth.

This became blatantly apparent when they penned the charters of those original thirteen colonies. They left their motivations for founding these colonies for all posterity to read and remember. Rhode Island was chartered in 1683 with the following words inscribed in her charter, "We submit our persons, our lives and our estates unto our Lord Jesus Christ, the King of Kings and the Lord of Lords, and to all those perfect and absolute laws given us in His Holy Word." In Maryland their charter read that they were "formed by a pious zeal to extend the Christian gospel." Not to be outdone, their neighbors in Delaware wrote in their charter that they were "formed for the further propagation of the gospel of the Lord Jesus Christ." And up in Connecticut they expressed in their charter that their colony's purpose was "to preserve the purity of the gospel of the Lord Jesus Christ." With talk of someday adding Washington, D.C. as a 51st state, I wonder how different her charter might read?

We have come a long way today. We have diverted from our founders' path so far that it is now common to see the federal courts repeatedly doing such things as restricting manger scenes from city squares and removing ten commandment displays from government buildings. Except those, I might add, where they are carved in granite like the Supreme Court building in Washington, D.C. itself.

Unfortunately, there are some alarming similarities between ancient Babylon and modern America. There is an expensive price to pay when any nation loses all sense of remembrance of who they are or from whence they have come.

THE DANGER OF LOSING ALL SENSE OF REALITY

"Belshazzar the king made a great feast for a thousand of his lords, and drank wine in the presence of the thousand."
(Daniel 5:1)

In order to understand how the king had lost all sense of reality around him, it must be remembered that outside the city walls of Babylon, the Medes and the Persians were encamped besieging the city. But inside, Belshazzar is partying. Here is presumption personified. The Babylonians began to think that because of their history of dominance and their strong walls they were invincible and indestructible. Those great walls stretched for sixty miles in circumference. But everywhere you looked along the top of them now you saw the enemy surrounding the city. But, no problem, they thought. After all, the walls were so high and thick they were impossible to penetrate and a twenty-year supply of rations lay inside.

So, what did Belshazzar do? He lost all sense of reality. He threw a big party and invited thousands of guests to his drunken orgy. His confidence was in the physical. His was an impregnable city, at least, so he thought. So he partied when destruction was at his door. It is often in those times when we feel most secure in our own strength that peril is most imminent and danger is most near.

While the armies of Cyrus encircled the city, Belshazzar, at the moment of his greatest danger, thought he could party his

troubles away. He is a picture of many today who think that because they have gotten away with it before they will do so forever. This king was too blind and drunk on his own success to realize that the strength of a kingdom, or an individual, is never on the outside but on the inside. Babylon soon fell because they had become corrupt on the inside with no more sense of remembrance or reality.

Some in our own Babylon seem to think our walls are impregnable, that somehow God needs America to carry out His plan on earth. After all, we have won all the world wars, the cold war is over, and we seem to be the only real superpower still standing in the world today. But, I believe God is saying to us today, "Let him who thinks he stands take heed lest he also fall" *(1 Corinthians 10:12).*

Like those in ancient Babylon, we are so often prone to think we, too, are invincible. But, remember the judgment of God came to Judah and she was called the "apple of His eye." There was a time when Israel was, herself, the world's only superpower. She was one nation under God. Her motto was "In God we trust." King David and King Solomon took her to superpower status. God gave her a land, a law, and a Lord.

Three thousand years after King David, God birthed another nation. God gave us a land. He gave us a law built and based on Israel's ancient commandments. And, He gave us a Lord to love and to live under. Why should we think we, too, are invincible when we lose our sense of remembrance and reality? Of Babylon, God said, "You have been weighed in the balance and found wanting" *(Daniel 5:26).* Is it not time for us to remember who we are and

from whence we have come? Is it not time for us to recapture the reality of what is taking place around us and truly pray, "God forgive us and God bless America" again?

THE DANGER OF LOSING ALL SENSE OF RESTRAINT

"While he tasted the wine, Belshazzar gave the command to bring the gold and silver vessels which his father, Nebuchadnezzar, had taken from the temple which had been in Jerusalem that the king and his lords, his wives and his concubines might drink from them." (Daniel 5:2)

When a nation, or an individual, loses all sense of remembrance and reality, it follows that they also lose all sense of restraint. The Babylonians were too blind to see any correlation between moral decay and national decline. Does this sound familiar at all? Daniel 5:2 describes what the Old Testament politely calls "concubines." These were women who were kept for the king's pleasure for the purpose of sexual gratification and additional procreation. Our nation, like Babylon, has been virtually given over to sexual permissiveness and perversions of all types.

The pages of this book are not voluminous enough to describe by way of illustration the various depictions of graphic sexual perversion that infiltrate this modern western culture twenty-four/seven through movies, television, print media, Internet and the like. In his book, *Our Dance Has Turned to Death,* Carl Wilson chronicles the pattern of decline of the Greco-Roman culture.

He observes that first, men began to cease to lead their own families in spiritual and moral development. Next, they neglected their wives and children in pursuit of material wealth and power. This was followed by men becoming so preoccupied with business ventures that they began to ignore their wives and become involved with other women outside the home. Thus, their wives began to seek their own worth and value outside the home and marriage laws eventually made divorce easier to come by. Then, because male and female role models were no longer prominent in the home, the children developed identity problems of their own. Finally, this left many children unwanted and, for the most part, undisciplined. I do not believe we need much in the way of application at this point. Now, two thousand years later, it is strangely descriptive of another culture we know all too well.

Belshazzar and the Babylonians had lost all sense of restraint. And, not just morally. Here we also see them in a spiritual debacle. They took what God called "Holy," the vessels of the temple, and desecrated them for their own godless satisfaction. God is still serious about anyone anywhere desecrating what He calls holy. God is weighing us on His balance today and I fear we, too, are being found wanting. Have we, too, lost all sense of restraint?

THE DANGER OF LOSING ALL
SENSE OF RESPECT

**"Then they brought the gold vessels that had been taken from
the temple of the house of God in Jerusalem; and the king and his
lords, his wives, and his concubines drank from them.
They drank wine, and praised the gods of gold and silver,
bronze and iron, wood and stone." (Daniel 5:3-4)**

Look at this crumbling culture of Babylon. Nothing was sacred
to them anymore. Because they had abandoned all absolutes,
it naturally followed that there were no restraints and, when
restraints are left behind, then there is found no respect for
anything that is sacred. It was party time in Babylon.

Then an amazing thing happens. "The fingers of a man's hand
appeared and wrote opposite the lamp stand on the plaster of
the wall" *(Daniel 5:5)*. The king sobered up. His "knees knocked
against each other" *(Daniel 5:7)*. Into the party hall comes Daniel
(Daniel 5:13). He was not at the party. Most people do not want the
man of God around when the liquor is flowing and the women
are present. But, when the writing is on the wall, when the crisis
comes, they no longer want their immoral friends and drinking
buddies, they are looking for someone who can tell them what
this means.

Daniel looked around the scene. The shouting and drinking
and sex had come to a stop. A strange silence filled the banquet
hall. People looked as if they were frozen in time. The sacred
vessels were scattered around the tables. Daniel was the only

one in that ballroom who was calm. He then did what every preacher should do. He took the Word that came from God and without fear or favor simply revealed to them all of what God had said. This is still the preacher's responsibility to this very day.

Listen to Daniel as he stands before them. Before he interpreted the handwriting on the wall, he preached a sermon to them with three points. First, there was a word about power. Daniel reminded Belshazzar that King Nebuchadnezzar's power came from God *(Daniel 5:18-19).* Second, there was a word about pride. Daniel reminded the king that Nebuchadnezzar lost his kingdom because of pride *(Daniel 5:20).* Third, there was a word about punishment *(Daniel 5:21).* King Nebuchadnezzar was punished until he came to realize that the "Most High rules in the kingdom of men, and gives it to whomever He chooses"*(Daniel 4:32).*

Next, Daniel applied the text. "You have not humbled yourself, although you knew all this" *(Daniel 5:22).* He said, "King Belshazzar, you knew about the power, the pride, and the punishment." Yet, sadly, he had lost all sense of remembrance, reality, restraint and respect.

When, and if, we forget these things ourselves, then we become blind to the fact that, like Babylon, our problems are not primarily political, economic or social. The decline of any nation has its roots in spiritual factors. All the other issues are simply symptomatic.

Back to the banquet. The hall is hushed. Daniel now reveals the handwriting on the wall. "Mene, Mene, Tekel, Upharsin" *(Daniel 5:25).* Daniel digs into the lexical roots of these words in

order to reveal the three elements involved in the sinner's doom. Numbered. Weighed. Separated. The end of opportunity, the Judgment, eternity.

Mene is from Aramaic meaning "numbered." That is, your number is up, your time has run out, you are finished, it is over. There are no more opportunities and no more second chances. And that is the way it happens. Suddenly. The finger of God writes on the wall, "Mene," when we least expect it. Yes, even in the midst of partying our way through life. Mene...your number is up.

Tekel is a word meaning "to weigh." The word picture is of a scale with God's standard on one side and you on the other. But you are too light. You do not measure up. God's standard is the law. Who of us has not been measured on this scale and found wanting apart from the righteousness of Christ in our behalf?

Upharsin means "to break into two pieces, to separate, to divide." The Lord was always doing this. He separated, divided, the sheep from the goats and the wheat from the tares.

Note the scene that evening in Babylon. The ballroom was now a scene of fright and terror but there was one figure who stood in perfect peace. There was no fright on his face and no concern on his countenance. He knew well the very One who had written on the wall. The Day of Judgment holds no fear for those, like Daniel, who know the Living God.

Daniel, chapter five, concludes with these very words, "That very night Belshazzar...was slain and Darius, the Mede, received the kingdom" *(Daniel 5:30-31)*. Yes, "that very night." While Babylon had partied with no sense of restraint or remembrance,

the armies of the Medes and the Persians diverted the Euphrates into swampland and the Persian army marched right into the city through the dry river bed that ran under the city walls and took the city.

God's judgment is sure. There are no walls high enough or thick enough to prevent a man, or a nation, from falling when God writes, "Mene, Tekel, Upharsin" on the wall.

Who really knows how close we might be to that word, "Mene," our time is up, our number is up? Or, who knows how close we might be to "Tekel," weighed in the balance and found wanting? Or, "Upharsin?" The kingdom is divided and separated from you.

Few nations have had a history like America. For over two hundred years we have been as a shining light to the world in many respects. We have been a launch pad to take the gospel literally to the very ends of the earth. We often hear people say, "God is our only hope." But, I wonder if God might not be our biggest threat! What is there about America that should offer us a special dispensation that neither Babylon nor even Ancient Israel were given?

There is a last night for every nation, and for every individual. In light of eternity what is the kingdom of Babylon or any other nation compared to the kingdom forfeited by men and women without Christ who shall be weighed and found wanting? Since our days are numbered, should we not sense the urgency to exchange our own righteousness for the righteousness of Christ through the new birth that we might not be found wanting in that day?

America has had some proud moments but none finer than that foggy morning of June 6, 1944. Those American boys approached the French coast at low tide. In wave after wave after wave they stormed the beaches of Normandy. Within one month over one million Allied troops had filled Europe and brought an end to the diabolical and murderous grip of Hitler's Germany. But, when we think about it, that was not the original D-Day. I once heard Max Lucado, the master wordsmith, in telling this story put it like this — "God established his own beachhead in Bethlehem. He triumphed over the strongest enemy. He used a woman, a baby, and a Bethlehem feeding trough." Christ is our hope!

On this Memorial Day, as we remember those who gave so much for the freedoms we enjoy today, may we be reminded anew that, in the words of Daniel, "The Most High still rules over the affairs of men" *(Daniel 4:32)*. And, may we bow our hearts and our knees before Him...and may God bless America!

[86]

CHAPTER VII.

F A T H E R ' S   D A Y

Luke 15:11-32

FATHER'S DAY...A TIME FOR NEW NECKTIES, FAMILY LUNCHES, LONG DISTANCE CALLS AND GREETING CARDS. It also affords us an opportunity to examine a model father, the kind of dad every kid deserves.

I had a dad who was very predictable. I remember him as being always there for me. In fact, I can hardly think of a "first" in my life that wasn't marked by his presence. He was there for my first breath...my first word...my first step...my first day of school... my first ball glove...my first car. My high school graduation, my college graduation, my seminary graduation all had his presence in common. Virtually every memory of my childhood and adolescence from vaccinations to vacations and from ball games to baccalaureates were all memorable experiences for me because of him. Growing up I never wondered or worried if the bills got paid, if the lawn got mowed or if we would have a roof over our heads. In an earlier chapter I wrote about our old family photo album. One might think it strange that there are not a lot of pictures of him to be found in it. He was always the one behind the camera making sure everyone else had a good time and that it was well documented in pictures.

Not everyone on this Father's Day is fortunate enough to have had a father like that. And then, I suppose, some who did might have even taken dad for granted. Some today will be a father someday themselves. Thus, I want to plant a seed in our minds about the kind of father every child deserves.

More and more we are evolving into a matriarchal society. God never intended for this. Today there are too many men who are opting to leave instead of love. Others have virtually abdicated their place of leadership in the home. The presence of a father is an integral key to the success of the home.

Quite honestly, there are not a lot of role models for fathers today. However, there is one who is tucked into one of the parables told by our Lord. He is often overlooked in the story due to the emphasis that is placed on one or the other of his two sons. We call them the prodigal son and the elder brother. I would venture to say that over 90% of the messages we hear on this passage of scripture have one of the two boys on center stage. Yet, the story is really not about them at all. It is about the father. Note how Jesus begins the parable, "A certain man had two sons" *(Luke 15:11)*. Who is the subject of the sentence? The sons? No, the father. He is on center stage here. He is the subject not only of the opening sentence but of the whole story.

Here is a picture of a model father from whom we can all learn some valuable lessons on this Father's Day. Look at him. He is foresighted. He is forbearing. He is forgiving. He is forgetful. And, he is focused. Let's not simply look at him today but learn from him some valuable life lessons.

THE MODEL FATHER
IS FORESIGHTED

"A certain man had two sons and the younger of them said to his father, 'Father, give me the portion of goods that falls to me.' So he divided to them his livelihood." (Luke 15:11-12)

The model father is foresighted. By this we mean that he knows that what he puts into his child at a young age is going to determine what he becomes and how he behaves in later years. Thus, he is an example himself and imparts into his son some absolutes.

The model father teaches the truth to his children from infancy through adolescence. Remember, Jesus was telling this story to Jews *(Luke 15:1-2)*. These were people who had a rich heritage in the Mosaic Law with its parental responsibilities well defined. Just before the children of Israel entered their Promised Land, Moses gathered them together and said, "These commandments that I give you today are to be upon your hearts. Impress them upon your children. Talk about them when you sit at home and when you walk along the road, when you lie down and when you get up. Tie them as symbols on your hands and bind them on your foreheads. Write them on the doorframes of your homes and on your gates" *(Deuteronomy 6:4-9)*.

The model father teaches his children the scripture. He is an example before them in life and lip. He is not merely a "hearer of the Word" but a "doer of the Word" before his family. He has the foresight to know that his actions speak even louder than his

words. He gives his children some absolutes. Thus, in the case of the father and his prodigal there are some moral values instilled there from which the son rebels at times.

If we are going to be the kind of father that any child deserves, then we need this type of foresight ourselves. We need to not simply be a material provider (that is important) and not simply a mental provider (and, that is important) but a moral provider as well, instilling scripture and absolutes into our children.

THE MODEL FATHER IS FORBEARING

"...he divided to them his livelihood..." (Luke 15:12-20)

The model father is forbearing. That is, he is restrained. He lets the boy go when the time comes *(Luke 15:12-13)*. He realizes that some sons seem to have to learn the hard way. This dad could have refused to let the boy go. He could have blackmailed him with the inheritance. He could have played the guilt game, "How could you do this to your mother and me?" There are times when the model father knows what is best but still lets his son go.

I am a dad myself. I have tried to put myself in his shoes as I have written this chapter. Here is a boy, after all his dad has done for him, who comes and thumbs his nose at his dad. This father could have played the comparison game, "Why can't you be like your older, obedient brother?" There are all sorts of games and innuendos that could have been played at this time.

But here we find a dad who, evidently, was prepared to stand by what he had put in that boy from childhood. He knew the truth of King Solomon's words that we should "train up a child in the way he should go and when he is old he will not turn from it" *(Proverbs 22:6)*. The key word here is "train." This promise is not for one who simply sends his child to Sunday School for one hour out of a 168-hour week. This is a promise to the dad who has "trained" his child by life and lip and love and through the investment of his most valuable commodity, his time.

The model father is not simply foresighted, he is forbearing. He restrained himself. He lets the boy become a man. Some dads never learn this. Some continue to hold their children so tightly that they lose them in the very process. This dad let the boy go. He didn't send one of his servants to spy on him. As much as his own heart was breaking and as much as he knew what hard lessons lay ahead for his son, he let him go. I wonder how many of us are willing to forbear, respect our children's autonomy when they have come of age, and are willing to release them. Yes, he let him go. But, he never gave up on him.

Many of us are tolerant up to a point. Then we somehow and so often lose our patience. This father just kept being faithful at home, living with a broken heart at times but never giving up. The boy left home to be free. But he became a slave to those things he thought would give him independence. This generally happens when we get outside the umbrella of authority God has placed in the home and in our lives.

I love the way verse 17 describes what happened. It says the boy "came to himself." All those years of loving training paid

off. The boy had been taught better and he knew it. And so, he heads for home hoping to simply become a hired servant.

I can almost see this dad now standing on his porch or perhaps working in the fields but always keeping an eye on the horizon, looking down that road in hopes the boy would come home. And the scripture says that finally one day, "While he was still a long way off the father saw him and was filled with compassion for him. He ran to his son, threw his arms around him and kissed him" *(Luke 15:20).* He never gave up.

THE MODEL FATHER IS FORGIVING

"...the father saw him and had compassion; and ran and fell on his neck and kissed him." (Luke 15:20)

Yes, the model father is forgiving. When the boy was a long way down that road, the father started running to him. The boy may have come walking but dad came running.

The boy began his speech *(Luke 15:15-18)* but he never got to give it. The father was full of forgiveness. What a dad! He ran to him with a warm welcome. There was no, "How could you have done this to us?" There was no, "Where have you been all this time?" There was no, "What did you do with the money?" There was no, "I hope you are happy now." There was no, "I told you so." There was only a warm, "Welcome home, son."

This dad had "compassion." This word comes from two Latin words which mean "to suffer with." Thus, dad knew what the boy had been through; he knew what was in his heart. The boy had come home hoping to become a hired servant and dad restored him in forgiveness to his rightful place as an honored son.

Yes, the kind of dad every child needs is not simply one who is foresighted and forbearing but one who is forgiving as well.

THE MODEL FATHER
IS FORGETFUL

"...bring the best robe...put a ring on his hand...kill the fatted calf...this, my son, was lost and now he is found..."
(Luke 15:22-24)

It is one thing to forgive but quite another to forget. This model father does not hold a grudge. He forgives...and he also forgets. He allows his boy a place of beginning again. He could have said, "Welcome home, son. I forgive you but you have got a lot of proving to do around here." But he didn't. He put it all behind him.

Now, to say that the model father forgets does not mean that there should be no rules in particular cases of certain prodigals' returns. Remember, we are not seeing a boy here in this story who came home with a rebellious spirit. What is the difference? We are witnessing a boy here who truly repented. He regretted

his deed. "He came to himself" *(Luke 15:17).* He blamed himself for his actions. Hear him say, "Father, I have sinned against heaven and before you and am no more worthy to be called your son" *(Luke 15:18).* He acknowledged his father's right to be displeased. He said, "I am no more worthy to be called your son" *(Luke 15:19).* And, he resolved in his heart to not repeat his mistake. "He arose and came to his father" *(Luke 15:20).*

Repentance involves a change of attitude which will result in a change of affections which results in a change of action. This process is beautifully illustrated in this boy's own repentance. First, he changed his mind, his attitude… "He came to himself." Next, this changed his will, his volition, his affections… He said, "I *will* arise and go to my father." And then, this led to a change in action… "He arose and went home." Here was a dad who could not simply forgive but forget because here was a son who came home with a truly repentant spirit.

When we forgive, we ought to forget. God does. Aren't we glad he doesn't deal with us "according to our sins" *(Psalm 103:10)* but according to "His tender mercies" *(Psalm 51:1)?* The model father is forgetful. And aren't we thankful?

THE MODEL FATHER IS FOCUSED

"…he (the elder brother) was angry and would not go in… you never gave me a young goat that I might make merry with my friends." (Luke 15:28-29)

The model father is focused. That is to say that he has his priorities in order and keeps things in proper perspective. Note that in verse 29, the sulking elder brother is complaining about never having been given a young goat as a party feast with his own friends. Think about that. We are talking here about the "fatted calf" *(Luke 15:23)*. To complain about never receiving a young goat at a time like this was sheer folly. This older brother had lost all sense of perspective. How fortunate were these boys to have had a dad who was focused on the right things.

The party is now in full swing. The festivities are at a high. But where is dad? No one can find him. He is outside with his older son helping him to get things in focus and proper perspective. He is assuring the older brother he is "always with him," that "all that I have is yours" and he is keeping the focus on the fact that it is right to party for the younger brother had been lost and now was found. The truth is, life goes on and so must we.

Ironically, we are never told how the story ends. The Lord just concludes it without our ever knowing what happened. Did the older brother go in to the party? We simply do not know. Perhaps our Lord left this shrouded in silence in order for you to finish the story yourself on this Father's Day.

This is a beautiful picture of a model father. But the real message on this special day is that this is really a picture of our own heavenly Father. He is foresighted…so much so that He knew that without a substitutionary sacrifice we could never make peace with ourselves or with God. Thus, He gave us not only some absolutes but the gift of His own Son that we might be born into His family.

Like the model father in Jesus' story our Heavenly Father is also forbearing. He lets us go. We are people, not puppets, and the love we can voluntarily return to Him is indescribably valuable to Him. And, He never gives up on us. He is forgiving and forgetful. In fact, He said, "I will forgive your iniquity and I will remember your sin no more" *(Jeremiah 31:34)*. And, He is focused. He has everything concerning us in proper perspective.

Isn't it time, on this Father's Day morning, that we complete this story? When we do, we will find Him just like the Prodigal Son found his father...with wide and forgiving open arms and the promise of a new beginning.

CHAPTER VIII.

STEWARDSHIP SUNDAY

Proverbs 3:9-10

THERE ARE MANY PASTORS AND CHURCHES THAT AVOID THE SUBJECT OF STEWARDSHIP LIKE A PLAGUE. In fact, many modern church gurus are telling pastors across the country not to talk about money or stewardship. I find that to be very strange since our Lord spoke of it in one-third of His parables. In the churches I was privileged to pastor, we made no apologies in challenging one another in the realm of stewardship for it was a great part of our own spiritual development and growth.

Money consumes us in our current culture. Many churches are full of financial planners, bankers, stockbrokers, money managers, venture capitalists, CPAs, lawyers and all kinds of men and women who are constantly giving financial counsel. How would you like the free counsel of a man recognized the world over as one of the richest, most successful and wisest men who ever lived? This particular man "wrote the book" on international commerce. In fact, of him it was said, "God gave (him) wisdom and exceedingly great understanding, and

largeness of heart like the sand on the seashore. Thus (his) wisdom excelled the wisdom of all the men of the East and all the wisdom of Egypt. For he was wiser than all men – than Ethan the Ezrahite, and Heman, Chalcol, and Darda, the sons of Mahol; and his fame was in all the surrounding nations. He spoke three thousand proverbs, and his songs were one thousand and five" *(I Kings 4:29-32).* His name? Solomon. Listen to his counsel on money management. "Honor the Lord with your possessions, and with the firstfruits of all your increase; so your barns will be filled with plenty, and your vats will overflow with new wine" *(Proverbs 3:9-10).*

As far-fetched as it might seem, our finances generally mark the position of our own spiritual pilgrimage. We are no farther along in our walk with the Lord than the point in which we learn to trust Him with the tithe.

There are a lot of questions regarding stewardship. How can we afford to return one-tenth of our income back to God? How much should we give? There are four questions every believer should ask about stewardship: (1) What is the purpose of my stewardship? (2) What is the product of my stewardship? (3) What is the priority of my stewardship? (4) What is the promise of my stewardship?

WHAT IS THE PURPOSE OF MY STEWARDSHIP?

"Honor the Lord…" Proverbs 3:9-10

What is the purpose when we attend a worship service and the offering plate is passed and we place our gift in it? Note the first three words of our text – "Honor the Lord." This should be our single most important goal in life – to honor God. It is always a good thing to check our motivation, our purpose regarding the issues of life. Honoring God should be our primary motive in everything we do, whether in our marriage, our social life, our business or whatever.

What is the purpose of our stewardship? Some are motivated by guilt. That is, they give because they think they ought to. Others are grudge givers. That is, they give because they think they have to. The New Testament teaches us to be grace givers – we give out of a heart of gratitude and love because we want to!

The Hebrew word that we translate into our English word "honor" is very enlightening at this point. What does it mean when we are exhorted to "honor God"? Often this word is used to describe the concept of being weighted down. For example, a king is weighted down with all the accessories of royalty – the crown, the robe, the train, the scepter, the medallion. When we honor God it means that we weigh Him down. Crown Him Lord! It is closely akin to what young people used to say, "That's heavy!" This being translated means, "That is incomprehensible, awesome, powerful." To say that we honor God means that we give Him His rightful place in our lives. He is Lord!

What is the purpose of our stewardship? Is it some lucky rabbit's foot? Is it that I give so that I might get, as some teach? Is it some legalistic Old Testament discipline that keeps me bound

to the law? Our purpose in stewardship has to do with honoring God by exhibiting trust in Him.

We are nothing more than stewards passing through this world. Fifty years from now everything you own will be in someone else's name. Fifty years ago what is in your name today was in someone else's; your land, your home, your assets. When you entered this world, you entered it naked without a dime, and you will leave it the same way. In reality, we do not own a thing. We are simply stewards. Therefore, it is imperative that we honor God with our possessions. This is our purpose in stewardship. God makes an incredible statement in I Samuel 2:30 when He says, "those who honor Me, I will honor." What is the purpose of our stewardship? It is to honor God!

WHAT IS THE PRODUCT OF MY STEWARDSHIP?

"...with your possessions..." Proverbs 3:9-10

We are to honor God. With what? Our possessions, our money, our wealth. Note the product of our stewardship is not just our time. It is not simply our talents. This is not what Solomon is saying. It is our treasure that is specifically addressed here. Some of us live as if our lives were a hotel corridor with room after room. As God walks down the hall, He sees the family room with the door open for Him to come in. He sees our social room, our work room, our exercise room, our activity room, our hobby room, and they are all open to Him. But in many lives when it

comes to the room where we have our possessions, our money, He sees a "Do Not Disturb" sign on that door. What is the one thing that is prone to dominate and dictate our lives? Money! In fact, God says in I Timothy 6:10 that "the love of money is a root of all kinds of evil." We get trapped by government policies and our own lifestyles into thinking that money is the answer to every problem. How many times have we asked someone how they were doing, only to have heard the reply that everything was okay and they had no problems that money would not solve! Thus, the Lord indicates an area of our lives which tells us more about our spiritual condition than any other. He says it is our possessions, and hence Solomon says, "Honor God with your possessions."

It is good to have things that money can buy. However, there is something better. It is to have what money cannot buy. As I write these words I am thinking back to the wedding ring I gave my wife, Susie. It is now in a stickpin. I was a student in 1970 and could only afford a small ring. I remember the salesman making a special deal on the particular ring I purchased because if you look closely enough you will see a big carbon spot in the middle of it. I would be embarrassed for her to know how little I paid for it. However, that ring symbolized a tremendous amount of love as well as the confidence that God had brought us together. At about the same time a college friend gave his fiancée one of the biggest, most beautiful diamond rings I have ever seen, worth thousands of dollars. The tragedy is that their marriage did not last a year. Money can buy a lot of things. It can buy million-dollar houses, but all the money in the world cannot

transform a house into a home. What is really important is not what money can buy, but what it cannot buy.

While some of us desire to honor God with our lives we never think of honoring Him with our possessions. How do we do this? There are three ways in which we honor God with our possessions. First, we honor God with how we *get* it. Some people get wealth in ways that are dishonoring to God.

We also can honor or dishonor God by the way we *guard* it. The Lord Jesus said in Matthew 6:19, "Do not lay up for yourselves treasures on earth." Many guard their wealth. Some even make arrangements to keep it hoarded and guarded even after they are gone. It is no accident that our last will is called our Last Will and Testament, or Testimony. It is the last opportunity we have to give our testimony to the world of what was really important to us. One day someone will read it and tell what really held your heart because Jesus said, "Where your treasure is, there your heart will be also" *(Matt. 6:21)*.

James spoke of a man who "hoarded" his wealth *(James 5:3)*. Guarded wealth brings no joy. Some people get their stock portfolios or checking and savings statements each month. No matter how much we have we wish it were just a little bit more. When we begin to love money, it ceases to bless us and begins to curse us. No wonder Solomon said, "Honor the Lord with your possessions."

God is as concerned with how we guard our wealth as He is with how we get it. Susie and I do not have a large estate after all these years of marriage. We have invested in the bank of heaven. Much of the savings of our first twenty years of marriage is in

the auditorium in Fort Lauderdale, Florida, where hundreds of people came to know Christ every year and from where dozens of missionaries have been sent. Our daughters know they are not going to get much from us. A large portion of what we will leave behind has already been designated to Mission:Dignity, our program to aid retired pastors or their widows living below the poverty level. We intend to leave our children something far more important than a pile of money to hoard or to guard or even to throw away. We have sought to teach them the importance of laying up treasures in heaven. Why? Because our heart always follows our treasure *(Matt. 6:21)*. If we wait until we feel like giving, we will never do it. The natural man wants to guard it. Thus Solomon gives us wise counsel when he says we are to "Honor God with our possessions."

We honor God by not only how we get and guard our money, but also with how we give it. We are stewards of God's blessing. How we give is vitally important. The Lord Jesus still sits over the treasuries to see how His people give. One day I will stand before this great God. He is not going to say to me, "Let me see your Bible." Quite frankly there is not a page in my Bible that is not marked and filled with notations. He is not going to look at me and ask, "Is your Bible all marked?" He is not going to say, "Let me see your sermon notebook. Are there any notes there?" I don't believe He is even going to ask for my prayer journal. Some of us may be shocked. I think He might say, "Let me see your checkbook; I want to look at your cancelled checks." Why? Because how we use what He gives us tells us where our heart is. He said, "Where your treasure is, there your heart will be also" *(Matt. 6:21).*

This is the purpose and product of our stewardship. The way we handle our possessions is so much a reflection of what is on the inside of us that our Lord Jesus Christ addressed it in one out of three of His recorded sermons and His parables.

WHAT IS THE PRIORITY OF MY STEWARDSHIP?

"…with the firstfruits of all your increase…" Proverbs 3:9-10

Note that Solomon is specific with the portion of our possessions with which we are to honor God. He calls it the "firstfruits." The Israelites brought the firstfruits of all their crops to God in order to acknowledge that He was the ultimate owner of the land. God said, "The land shall not be sold permanently, for the land is Mine; for you are strangers and sojourners with Me" *(Lev. 25:23)*. God owns the land of Israel today, and by His grace Israel is His tenant. Thus as they brought the firstfruits offerings they were honoring Yahweh. Should we do less?

The first portion of everything we own should be set aside for God's use. The Old and the New Testament both refer to it as the tithe – one-tenth of our income. The New Testament pattern is characterized by freedom. But freedom does not negate the validity of the tithe. *The Believer's Study Bible* note says, "Tithing is only the beginning place of Christian stewardship, not the end. God does not want you to give less than a tithe, but He may want you to give so much more through His enabling grace."

For me personally, I have never felt that in this dispensation of grace that I should give less than the Jews gave under the dispensation of the law. Hence, tithing is only the beginning place, the firstfruits.

In his own inimitable way, Dr. W.A. Criswell frames this point with these words, "Four hundred years before the law was given, Father Abraham paid tithes to Melchizedek, priest to the most high God. Tithing was the foundation of supportive worship of the Israelites throughout the dispensation of the law. It was in that era that the Lord Jesus lived and had His being. It was He who said we ought to tithe *(Matt. 23:23).* In this dispensation in which you and I live, it is the Lord Jesus Christ who received our tithes even though our human hands take it up in the congregation. Hebrews 7:8 says, "Here mortal men receive tithes, but there He received them, of whom it is witnessed that He lives." There is a sense in which every time we receive an offering in church, although mortal men are serving as ushers to receive the gifts, it is the Lord Jesus Christ Himself who is receiving them.

What is the priority of our stewardship? We are to honor God. With what? Our wealth. And what part of it? Firstfruits. I well remember the day my pastor, W. Fred Swank, taught me this truth. I was a student at Southwestern Seminary and serving as assistant pastor at Sagamore Hill Baptist Church in Fort Worth, Texas. I was about to be married, and Dr. Swank called me into his office on a particular day. He was known for always being blunt and to the point. He said, "Son, your giving has been a bit sporadic." With those words I knew I was about to learn a lesson. Those of us who were "his boys" never got away with

anything! I quickly replied, "Preacher, I am trying to tithe, but I get to the end of the month, and it just seems like there is not enough there." He looked at me and said, "We are to honor God with our possessions, with the firstfruits of all our increase." He continued, "Now, let me see your checkbook." Reluctantly I handed it to him. He asked another question, "What is fruit?" "That which you earn," I quickly replied. He countered, "What does *first* mean?" "First means first, the front of the line!" "Then, when you deposit your check on the first and fifteenth of each month make sure from now on the first check you write is the Lord's tithe, the firstfruits of all your increase," he said. He went on to explain to me that giving is an act of faith and showed me the meaning of Proverbs 3:5-6 which says we are to "trust the Lord with all of our hearts and lean not unto our own understanding. In all our ways acknowledge Him and He will direct our paths."

Since that day years ago I have never deposited a paycheck except that the first check I wrote after it was "unto the Lord," the firstfruit. Many years ago, Susie and I discovered the joy of giving way over the tithe every year of our married life. We did it when we had little or nothing. We did it when we were struggling with a young family. And we did it when we were responsible for college tuition, graduate school tuition and weddings. We still are blessed by it. It is the priority of our stewardship.

I am often asked by people who are contemplating becoming tithers if the tithe is to be given before or after taxes. For me, I never even considered the fact that taxes to a human government should be the firstfruits. To me the issue is plain. Solomon said, "Firstfruits" – of what? "All your increase." That is how we honor

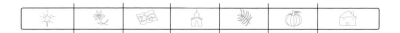

God. This is the priority of our stewardship. If we wait until we think we can afford it and continue to give our firstfruits to ourselves, or to others, or to our own pleasures, it won't happen. An unknown poet framed it best when he or she said,

The groom bent with age leaned over his cane

his steps uncertain needed guiding,

while down the church aisle

with a warm toothless smile

the bride in a wheelchair came riding.

Who is this elderly couple thus wed?

We've learned when we quickly explored it,

That this is that rare most conservative pair

Who waited till they could afford it!

Our purpose in life is to honor God. With what? With our possessions. And what part of our possessions? The "firstfruits" of all our possessions. There is one other question of stewardship that all of us should be asking:

WHAT IS THE PROMISE OF MY STEWARDSHIP?

"...so that your barns may be filled and your vats overflow with new wine." (Proverbs 3:9-10)

Full and overflowing! This is a far cry from the haunting call of many today – "Not enough." Here we see the John 6 principle in action. The boy gave his little lunch of loaves and fish. Thousands of people were fed and twelve baskets remained. In the words of Solomon, "Your barns will be filled with plenty and your vats will overflow with new wine." This is an amazing thought we find in Proverbs 3:10, "So your barns will be filled with plenty, and your vats will overflow with new wine." It is supernatural. I don't know how it works; I just know that after doing it every week for several decades, it does work. In fact, the word "be filled" in verse 10 is in the imperfect tense. It is an ongoing process. It just continues to be true as I continue to honor God with my possessions, with the firstfruits of all my increase. He just keeps on and on filling my barns.

Have you noticed that when God addresses our stewardship in

the Bible, His emphasis is not on our giving, but on our receiving? Malachi says, "Bring all the tithes into the storehouse, that there may be food in My house, and try Me now in this," says the Lord of hosts, "If I will not open for you the windows of heaven and pour out for you such a blessing that there will not be room enough to receive it" *(Mal. 3:10)*. The emphasis is on our receiving. In Proverbs 3:9-10 once again the emphasis is not on our giving as much as it is on our barns being filled – our receiving. In the New Testament, Jesus said it like this, "Give, and it will be given to you: good measure, pressed down, shaken together, and running over will be put into your bosom. For with the same measure that you use, it will be measured back to you" *(Luke 6:38)*. God's emphasis is always on our receiving, not so much on our giving. Solomon's statement in Proverbs 3:10 about our barns being filled is an incredible statement. It all boils down to one question, "Who are we going to believe?"

We have the wisest advice ever given on stewardship by the wisest man who ever lived. He put it like this, "Honor the Lord with your possessions, and with the firstfruits of all your increase; so your barns will be filled with plenty, and your vats will overflow with new wine" *(Prov. 3:9-10)*. What is the purpose of our stewardship? Are we simply trying to be a steward of our time and talent and not with our treasure? God said the product of our stewardship is "our possessions." What is the priority of our stewardship? Remember, the firstfruits belong to Him. What is the promise of our stewardship? We can take Him at His word. However, the real question is not if we ask ourselves these four questions, but if we will act upon them. If we have not been

regular tithers, will we begin to do so now?

The greatest stewardship verse in all the Bible is found in John 3:16, *"For God so loved the world that he gave His only begotten Son, that whoever believes in Him should not perish but have everlasting life."* The Lord Jesus was the product of the Father's stewardship to you. He was His only Son, the firstfruits of all those who would be born again after Him. We have a tremendous opportunity to honor God with our lives – the greatest of all our possessions. He said, "Those who honor Me, I will honor" *(I Sam. 2:30).*

CHAPTER IX.

WORLD MISSIONS DAY

Acts 16:10

WORLD MISSIONS IS THE VERY HEARTBEAT OF GOD. The Lord Jesus came "on mission" to our world when He clothed Himself in flesh and walked among us. The early first century church was a missionary church. The great Apostle Paul was not a theologian who became a missionary. He was first and foremost a missionary who was also a theologian.

God is still sending His people to the ends of the earth on missionary assignments today. He still calls particular people to particular places for particular purposes. Sadly, it has become strange in our modern day that "calling out the called" has become a foreign concept. Fewer and fewer congregations extend public invitations today and even among those who still do, there is seldom any appeal to "surrender" our lives to God's call to service.

As I read and reread many of the great missionary passages of the Bible recently, I became captivated by a phrase found in the account of Paul's second missionary journey. The phrase says, "After he had seen the vision" *(Acts 16:10)*. In this passage Paul sensed the call on his life to take the gospel to Europe.

He had returned from his first missionary journey and had written a letter back to the churches he had established along the way. We call this letter "Galatians" in our New Testament. Then, in Acts 15, Paul journeys to Jerusalem for the great church council. Twenty years had now passed since Pentecost. The issue was whether the Gentiles must follow various components of the Jewish ceremonial laws in order to be saved. Paul eloquently argued his case and the church settled the issue that salvation was indeed, by grace through faith in Christ alone.

After the Jerusalem Conference, Paul sensed the call to another missionary journey *(Acts 15:36-39).* Here we see a dispute arise between him and his missionary companion, Barnabas. The issue arose over whether young John Mark, who had left and returned home on the first journey, should accompany them on the second. Paul said no. Barnabas said yes. Who was right? In a sense they were both right. Paul's focus was on the *mission.* He was focused, single minded. He reasoned that if his young colleague had left before, he would do so again. After all, it was Jesus who had said that "no one putting his hand to the plow and looking back was fit for the kingdom." On the other hand, Barnabas' focus was on the *man.* Sure John Mark had failed. But, who hasn't? Barnabas was living up to his name (Son of Encouragement). The church of the Lord Jesus needs both of these men. Thus, they split up. Paul took Silas. Barnabas took John Mark. And they both followed God's call to missions *(Acts 15:40-16:5).*

Then, an amazing thing happens. As Paul went on his way, he was "forbidden by the Holy Spirit to preach the word in Asia. After they had come to Mysia they tried to go

into Bithynia, but the Spirit did not permit them. So passing by Mysia they came down to Troas" *(Acts 16:6-8).* Paul met one closed door after another. But he kept on the move. He kept moving forward. There was no rebuke because he tried to go to these other places. And then it happened... "A vision appeared to Paul in the night. A man of Macedonia stood and pleaded with him, saying 'Come over to Macedonia and help us'" *(Acts 16:9).* And then the phrase—"After he had seen the vision"—he went straight to his place of calling.

The question on this World Missions Day is, "Have you seen the vision, the calling of God?" Have we seen the vision of our world? We are part of a global community that now numbers well in excess of six billion people, every one of whom is formed and fashioned by God. We who live in America make up a little more than 4% of this number. When you break this equation down into observable and identifiable components, it is alarming. Look at your particular congregation next Sunday. If there are 200 people sitting in the pews, then look at eight of them. Yes, just eight. That is an object lesson of how many people are in our world outside our own borders. If your crowd numbers 1,000, then look at forty of them. Those approximately four pews represent the proportion of Americans to the world population. While you are looking at these congregations observe that of the crowd of 200, 48 of them would represent how many people are living in China alone and 36 of them would represent the people of India. It is also alarming to think that half of the world's wealth exists in those eight people in relationship to the crowd of 200. Those eight people representing the United States have a

life expectancy of over 75 years while the rest of the world's life expectancy is barely 40 years of age. And their garbage disposals digest more food daily than eighty percent of the world's men, women and children.

What must God think about those eight of us who figuratively sit in that congregation of two hundred? We are so blessed. Some of us think we are making a great sacrifice to invest one hour of our week in worship. The great commission is for the entire world. One of the fallacies of the modern "seeker friendly" church movement today is that so much of it is centered in self-interest and self-fulfillment. How can it be that 95% of those God is calling into ministry today are expecting to spend their time with those eight blessed people instead of the rest of the world?

Have you caught the vision? It was not until "after he had seen the vision" *(Acts 16:10)* that Paul headed out to what was then "the ends of the earth." Before every great spiritual accomplishment, God gives a vision for the task ahead. When He called Abraham He gave him a vision that his seed would be as "the stars" of the sky. When He called Joseph He gave him a vision of the crops bowing before him. Have you caught the vision God has for you and the job He has for you to do that no one else can do quite like you can?

It is also important to observe that after Paul had received the vision, "immediately" *(Acts 16:10)* he set out on his missionary journey. Some never know a missionary heart because they have no vision of the missionary heart of God. The vision for missionary service is still being given by the Father. We will

catch the vision and "call out the called" when we realize the Macedonian call to missions is as much for us today as it was to those in the early church.

THE MACEDONIAN CALL TO MISSIONS IS PERSONAL

"A vision appeared to Paul…" (Acts 16:9)

Note this particular call was personal. It was given "to Paul." God deals with us on a personal level. His vision for the better use of our gifts is personal. He still calls particular people to particular places for particular purposes. The only thing that keeps a lot of missionaries in the field in certain situations is the personal call of God to a particular place. God has a way of giving a vision for the task ahead and one man or one woman conceives it with Him, gestates it a while and later births it into reality.

The Macedonian call to world missions is personal. But it is of interest to note how it came to Paul. It did not come while he was hiding somewhere in a cave waiting for it. It did not come when he was sitting around like a monk somewhere waiting "to hear from God." It came to him when he was active. It came when he was on the move. It came when he was moving forward. It came when he was "risking his life for the name of the Lord Jesus Christ" *(Acts 15:26)* and when he

was making ready to go back and visit those he had seen on his first missionary journey to "see how they are doing"(*Acts 16:36*). And thus we find him going through Phrygia, Galatia, to the door of Asia, and then to Mysia, to Bithynia and finally to Troas *(Acts 16:6-8)*. He was on the move.

Have you caught the vision? Most usually it comes to people who are doing something, who are on the move themselves, who are active. This Macedonian call to missions is, first of all, personal. It was "to Paul." Perhaps it is to you.

THE MACEDONIAN CALL TO MISSIONS IS PRESSING

"A man from Macedonia stood and pleaded with him, saying, 'Come over to Macedonia and help us.'" (Acts 16:9)

Paul saw the vision of a man who "pleaded" with him for help. The word translates a Greek word, παρακαλεω, which means to encourage strongly, or to beseech with strong force. This present active participle indicates that the tense is continuous. That is, this man in Paul's vision kept standing before him, he kept pleading with him, he kept saying, "Come over and help us....come over and help us...come over and help us." This call is not simply personal, it is pressing.

The Macedonian call is an urgent one. Our world is waiting. Millions in their own quiet ways are "pleading" today for God's people to "come over and help us." And they are not just on the

other side of the world; some of them are right down the street. Over there in that transitional neighborhood is a single mother trying to work and raise her kids at the same time. She has been deserted. They are selling crack cocaine on her corner. One of the few role models her son has is the guy with the fancy car, the big gold chains around his neck and the chrome revolver in his pocket. She is pleading, "Come over and help me." The call to missions is pressing.

Somewhere out there today is a small child barely a dozen years of age. She comes home from school to take care of little brothers and sisters, to fix dinner, to wash and clean. Her mom is working two jobs. She has never known her dad. Can you hear her pleading, "Come over and help me?"

There is also a teenager out there somewhere today trying to cope with a mother who brings a different man home every weekend. Can you hear her pleading for help? Have you caught the Macedonian vision?

What about that young boy sitting at the lunch table by himself at school. No one seems to care and no one pays attention to him at school…or at home. He has never felt a mother's arms around him much less tuck him into bed at night. He has never heard his dad tell him he is proud to be his dad. In his own way he is pleading, "Come over and help me."

And what about that jail building we pass by on our way to work? In one of those cells is a man marking off "X's" on a calendar. He is sick and tired and about to give up hope. Can you hear him say, "Please, come over and help me"?

In that high-rise office sitting behind that big mahogany desk is a man with everything materially the world has to offer, except peace in his own heart. All his money and influence cannot keep his son away from dope or buy him happiness. His life is coming apart at the seams. In his own way he pleads, "Come over and help me."

And these stories could be multiplied many times over by the young mother who lies dying of AIDS in Africa, the father scrounging for food in the gutter to feed his starving family in some Indian metropolis. Or, a myriad of other similar circumstances and situations. People all over the world are pleading, "Come over and help us."

Have you caught the vision? Have you heard the Macedonian call to missions? You will when you begin to realize it is personal and pressing.

THE MACEDONIAN CALL TO MISSIONS IS PRECISE

"…a man from Macedonia…" (Acts 16:9)

There is not only a "who" and a "when" in the call of God to missions but there is also a "where." Paul's call was precise. It was to "Macedonia." Each of us should ask ourselves where Macedonia (the will of God) is for us.

Have you heard the Macedonian call? Do you know the voice of God when He speaks to your heart by His Spirit and through

His word? When I was a boy living on the East Side of Fort Worth I was usually playing ball on the old vacant lot up the street about dinnertime each evening. I can still hear my Mom's voice echoing out through that kitchen door shouting, "It is time to eat!" I knew my mother's voice. She didn't have to say, "This is your mother. Come to 3237 Crenshaw to the kitchen table." I knew she was speaking precisely to me and not to Steve or Jerry or any of the other kids on our block. How did I know her voice? I heard it every day. I recognized it. I listened to it. I obeyed it. Jesus said, "My sheep hear my voice…and I know them…and they follow me" *(John 10:3-4)*.

This precise calling for Paul to come to Macedonia was one of the turning points of human history. Macedonia was Europe. Had Paul turned eastward to Asia instead of westward to Europe, it would have resulted in a profound difference in world history. The European continent became the center of Christianity. Thus Paul headed west, on to Macedonia, to Philippi, to Thessalonica, then to Corinth and Athens and eventually Rome would lay ahead for him.

Have you caught the vision? It is personal, pressing and precise.

THE MACEDONIAN CALL TO MISSIONS IS PRACTICAL

"…help us…" (Acts 16:9)

We are not called to sit, but to go. There is not only a "who," a "when" and a "where" in the Macedonian call but there is

also a "what." The vision is a practical one. Our missionaries and the multitudes of people they are serving around the world today need help.

This man of Macedonia in Paul's vision was calling for "help." I have personally seen this call for help in the very faces of men, women and children around the world. I have seen it in the face of a little child in the slums of Nairobi. I have seen it in the face of a Palestinian teenager in the refugee camps of Bethlehem. I have seen it in the tattooed face of a woman who once was a sorcerer but who now sings praises to God under a tin roof in a bush church in East Africa. I have seen it in the toothless smile of an old Masai warrior in the Kenyan bush. I have seen it in the blank stares of the masses in China. I have seen it in the empty look of a little orphan girl in Romania.

"Come over and help us" is the cry of our world. We have a huge world. I once heard my missionary friend, Tom Elliff, ask, "If you saw a large long telephone pole with ten men carrying it on one end and one man lifting the other end, where would you go to help carry the pole?" The American church should be asking herself why it is that 95% of those called to ministry in her churches stay here to preach the gospel while the whole world is calling, "Come over and help us."

I have a growing sense that one of the lost passions of the modern pastor is the failure to "call out the called." This is seldom ever mentioned. Thus, young men and women and older ones alike are not being challenged to ask what Paul asked on the Damascus Road, "Lord, what would you have me to do?" The Macedonian call to missions is a very practical one.

THE MACEDONIAN CALL TO MISSIONS IS PROVIDENTIAL

"...we sought to go to Macedonia, concluding that the Lord had called us..." (Acts 16:10)

What a conclusion... "Concluding that the Lord had called us." There is something very interesting here. Paul was a spiritually led man with a sensitive heart who followed the Spirit's leading. When he was refrained from preaching in Asia *(Acts 16:6-8)* he did not wring his hands and say, "Well, I tried. It was just not what I thought it would be like." He kept on the move. He kept putting his hand on the next doorknob and when it would not open he went on to the next one. Some today seem to think they should simply sit and wait on their call. Some even quit the journey when they get to their own "Bithynia" and the door is shut. What is the moral here? When you sense the opportunity to show concern for others, move out, and go forward and the Lord will be with you.

God's call did not come to Paul when he was holed up in a cave somewhere. He was no monk. He was no hermit. He was on the move. God was leading him. Incidentally, note that there was no divine rebuke when he tried to go to Asia or Mysia or Bithynia or Troas. God's timing was just not right. Later, he would make his way through those doors, including to Ephesus. But it was not in God's timing as yet.

There is a key word in understanding this providential call here in verse ten. It reveals that he went on to Macedonia "concluding

that the Lord had called us." This word "concluding" translates the Greek word, συμβιβαζω. It means "to come together" just as a sweater being knitted does not look like much until it is folded over and finally knitted together and it "comes together." It is the picture of a jigsaw puzzle that doesn't look like much and then a piece fits here and another there and it begins to "come together." In other words, in Paul's mind, it all came together. The vision, this missionary call, was a confirmation of God's moving in his own life.

Here in this verse we see the truth of Isaiah when he said, "Whether you turn to the left or the right you will hear a voice behind you saying, 'This is the way, walk in it' " *(Isaiah 30:21)*. You will hear a voice. Where? Behind you. The only way this can be done is if you are on the move, doing what is right. This has happened in my own experience when I have headed in a direction and sensed that "still small voice" in my heart saying, "This is right." Often it comes in the way of a sense of peace, a release of conflict. And, it is accompanied by confirmation from His word.

Some today seem to want to be struck by lightning, so to speak, before they hear His call. No. Move out. Do something. Go somewhere. If it is not His will for you at that time, the door will close as it did for Paul at various places along his own journey. If it is His will, it will all "come together" and you too can "conclude that God has called you." Everyone I know who has been called and used by God heard the call, caught the vision, while they were on the move for and with the Lord and not while they were sitting and waiting for God to tell them

what to do. My own call to ministry occurred the summer before my senior year in college when I was "on the go" in Mexico on a mission trip.

Have you caught the vision? It is personal. It is pressing. It is precise. It is practical. And, it is also providential.

THE MACEDONIAN CALL TO MISSIONS IS POINTED

"…the Lord had called us to preach the gospel to them."
(Acts 16:10)

This is our primary purpose for Christian missions…"to preach the gospel to them." This is a pointed call. We are not primarily to build hospitals or schools, to erect orphanages, to teach agricultural principles or any of a thousand other very worthwhile aspects of mission work. All of these should be done with the primary purpose of "preaching the gospel."

A few years later this same Apostle Paul would write to the Romans and refer to himself as one who was "separated unto the gospel"*(Romans 1:1)*. The divine call of God upon our lives is one that truly separates us unto the gospel. It is pointed. Every other ambition or desire is to be relegated down the priority list of life and the extension of the gospel to the ends of the earth must remain our pointed priority.

No organization in the church has a right to exist unless its primary purpose is to extend the gospel message. The gospel is

defined for us in 1 Corinthians 15:3-4 in saying that "Christ died for our sins according to the scriptures, and He was buried, and He arose again on the third day according to the scriptures."

The phrase, "preach the gospel" *(Acts 16:10)* translates one word in Greek, ευαγγελιζω. It means to share the good news, this gospel story, and to do so in a way that it calls for a decision. We are not simply to find the prodigal son out in the pigpen, then organize a team to build a roof over his head while others find him some adequate clothes and still others take him a hot meal on wheels each day. Our task is to get that boy to "come to himself" *(Luke 15:17)* and to get him back to the Father's house. Once there, if we recall, it is his father who begins to meet his every need when he returns with a repentant and contrite heart.

This is the church's vision; this is our calling, to "preach the gospel to them." The Macedonian call to missions is a pointed and specific call.

THE MACEDONIAN CALL TO MISSIONS IS PROMPT

"...immediately we sought to go to Macedonia..." (Acts 16:10)

The Lord has given many a believer a vision that died because they did not act promptly in obedience to it. Not Paul... "Immediately" he set out. Even though some sense the call is personal, pressing and even precise, they – for whatever reason – delay the call and it never comes to fruition.

Note Paul's immediate response to the missionary call. There was no delay. "Immediately…" There was no doubt. "Immediately…" There was no defiance. "Immediately…"

There is a very subtle yet very interesting thing taking place here in verse ten. Note the change of pronouns from "they" to "we." Back in verse 8 we read, "so passing by Mysia *they* came down to Troas." Then in verse ten we read, "After *he* had seen the vision, immediately we sought to go to Macedonia." What happened? No doubt that Luke, the writer of Acts, had joined up with Paul at Troas and now begins giving a first-person report. Then, we read later in Acts 17:1 that the pronouns change back to "they" again. This, no doubt, indicates that Luke stayed in Philippi to establish and minister to the new church that was founded in that city.

Some of you may be hearing the Macedonian call to missions today. All that is left to do is to act promptly upon it. God will have his own way of seeing that others join you in the journey as happens here in Paul's own experience.

THE MACEDONIAN CALL TO MISSIONS IS PRODUCTIVE

"…we ran a straight course…to Philippi" (Acts 16:11-12)

Philippi. Talk about a productive response to the call of God. There is nothing like being in the middle of the will of God for our lives by responding with prompt obedience to His call.

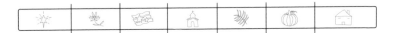

This journey across the Aegean from Troas to Philippi is a fitting conclusion to this chapter of Paul's story. Here Luke uses a Greek nautical term, ευθυδρομεω, which we translate "ran a straight course." What does it mean? Those who have sailed know that when the wind is in your face you have to zigzag across the lake to make any forward progress. But, when the wind is at your back, you can run a course to the other side that is straight as an arrow. You can just set the sail and go full speed ahead on a straight line.

Here in verse 11 we are seeing that the wind was at their back. And in more ways than one! When we catch the vision, get in the will of God and go forward, the wind of the Spirit is at our back guiding us and pushing us forward. Is it any wonder that those in life who continually try to sail against the wind of the Spirit never run "a straight course"?

Paul went to Macedonia, to Philippi. His first converts were a business woman named Lydia and an unnamed jailer. They became the pillars of the newly founded church there and this church financially supported the great Apostle the rest of his life and ministry. And, some twelve years later, he would write them a letter from his prison cell in Rome speaking to them of a life of continual rejoicing. We call this letter Philippians in our New Testament. And, it all began when he "caught the vision and concluded it was the will of God." And it so obviously was. When we trust and obey, we too find that the Macedonian call to missions is a most productive call.

So, this brings us to a final question. Have you caught the vision? There is nothing like being in the middle of the will of

God. Move out, do something, and "whether you go to the left or the right" you too "will hear a voice behind you saying, 'This is the way, walk in it'"(Isaiah 30:21). And, then you can join Paul in "concluding that this is the will of God" for you.

Yes, the old hymn still rings true today:

We have heard the Macedonian call today

"Send the light! Send the light!"

And a golden offering at the cross we lay

Send the light! Send the light!

Let us not grow weary in the work of love

"Send the light! Send the light!"

Let us gather jewels for a crown above

Send the light! Send the light!

Send the light, the blessed Gospel light

Let it shine from shore to shore!

Send the light, the blessed Gospel light

Let it shine forevermore!

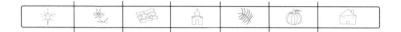

CHAPTER X.

C H R I S T M A S   E V E

Hebrews 10:5-7

ALL OVER OUR WORLD CHURCHES SPEND MUCH OF DECEMBER IN PREPARATION FOR PAGEANTS AND PLAYS ON CHRISTMAS EVE. During our years of pastoring in Fort Lauderdale our church began a Christmas pageant that through the years grew to mammoth proportions. But, I must confess that I much prefer the simple Christmas plays conducted by the thousands of smaller churches each Christmas Eve. There is beauty and dignity not only in the simple and oft-repeated story but also in the simplicity of crude props, terrycloth bathrobes serving as Shepherds' robes and a plastic baby doll placed in a crib of hay and stubble. There is just something that seems to be atmospheric about Christmas Eve.

I always found it amazing how much went on backstage before the curtain ever rises in a Christmas presentation. There are props to be made. There are costumes to be sewn. There is child care to be provided for the cast. There are faces to be made up and platforms to be constructed. There is music to be rehearsed

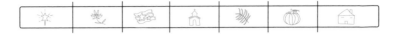

and lines to be memorized. It can be somewhat confusing, often complicated and sometimes even comical backstage.

But on this Christmas Eve when everything is focused on Bethlehem and the manger I would like for us to think a moment about what it must have been like backstage...backstage in heaven, that is. Backstage in heaven our Lord was speaking a farewell to the Old Testament saints, to the angels and to the Father. He, then, laid aside His glory, stepped over the portals of heaven and into the dung of a smelly Eastern stable.

What would He say to the Father as He departed? Before the curtain rose on the greatest event in all of human history what was the conversation backstage in heaven? Fortunately, the Bible has recorded it for us in Hebrews 10:5-7, "Therefore, when He came into the world He said, 'Sacrifice and offering You did not desire, but a body You have prepared for Me. In burnt offerings and sacrifices for sin You had no pleasure.' Then I said, 'I have come—in the volume of the book it is written of Me—to do Your will O God.'"

Now, that for which heaven had been waiting was coming. Now, that One to whom the prophets had been pointing was coming. The Father had been bringing to light the picture of His coming for generations. Way back in the early verses of Genesis the sun of His revelation began to rise casting its shadow for all to see. He was there pictured in the skins that clothed Adam and Eve, in righteous Abel's offering, Isaac's sacrificial lamb, in the Passover lamb of Egypt and in Isaiah's fifty-third chapter. Now, on Christmas Eve, it is high noon on God's clock of revelation. No more shadows. It is now "the fullness of time" and God was sending forth His own son. God, Himself, now clothed in human flesh, was stepping out of heaven and into human history. How? With "a body You have prepared for me." Why? "To do your will O God."

Christmas Eve in heaven…what a thought! Most of our thoughts on Christmas Eve are centered around what took place on earth. The Innkeeper. Joseph. Mary. Elizabeth. Zacharias. The stable. The shepherds. The wise men. The angels. But, what about Christmas Eve in heaven? Gabriel had returned from his visit and had made his report of Mary's response upon hearing the news. "My soul magnifies the Lord," she said. He reported on how faithful and obedient Joseph was while knowing that he would most likely become the brunt of every barroom joke in Nazareth. He told of the shepherds and their own excitement out in the fields of Bethlehem.

All of heaven was now looking over those portals. The "fullness of time" *(Galatians 4:4)* had come. Even though those on earth were mostly oblivious to this remarkable event, those in heaven were waiting, watching and worshipping.

Abel was looking over those portals. He had brought, not a work of his hands, but a sacrificial animal to the altar of worship and God had accepted it. "Now, I see it clearly," he declares. Abraham was looking over those portals. He had left the land of his father and now he watches Christ make ready to do the same. Isaac was peering over the portals also on that Christmas Eve. He had put the wood on his back and carried it up Moriah to be sacrificed himself. Now, he too, sees it more clearly. Moses was watching. He had taken the Passover Lamb and spread its blood

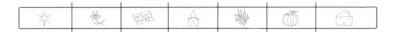

over the doorpost and lintel of the home and found out what it meant to be delivered from death and slavery. Rahab leaned over the portals that Christmas Eve also. Centuries earlier she had hung the scarlet thread out her window, a picture of Christ and His deliverance for us. And, Isaiah, he was certainly attentive. It was he who had prophesied that "a virgin would conceive" and would give birth to a Son who would later be "wounded for our transgressions."

And thus, backstage on Christmas Eve, the Lord Jesus turned to the Father and said, "A body You have prepared for me....I go now to do Your will." In these words we find two very important affirmations on this Christmas Eve. There is a word of condescension and a word of comprehension. Let's go backstage in heaven and listen in on this Christmas Eve conversation.

A WORD OF CONDESCENSION

"...a body You have prepared for Me..." (Hebrews 10:5)

What a step—from the splendor of heaven to the womb of a woman and finally to the stable of Bethlehem. There is so much behind this statement of our Lord, "A body you have prepared for me." The word "body" in the language of the New Testament translates a word meaning "material substance." We know well the Bible teaches that God is a Spirit. Thus, what a word of condescension we find here. This great creator God stepped into a body of flesh to identify with us. In this body He would become our own sin bearer.

There is much revealed in the use of the word "prepared" in this statement of our Lord. It translates a Greek word, καταρτιζω, which means to be framed or to be perfectly joined together. It is found here in the middle voice which simply means that the subject performs the action upon himself. What a divine revelation—this is God who took upon Himself a body.

Here is condescension of the first and finest order. He became as helpless as a tiny seed planted in a young girl's womb and as helpless as a little baby in total dependence upon someone else. He visited us and He did so as a baby. What condescension. His birth was unlike any other and yet, it was like ours in that it was accompanied by pain and struggle. He was born…not with the decency of a sterile environment with clean sheets…but in the dung and filth of a stable where sickness and death were likely possibilities.

Look at Mary. She is in labor. Her back is aching. Her feet are swollen. She is sweating. She is having contractions. The little babe's head pushes itself into the world. She is struggling, pushing. And then, He arrives! God in flesh has come to visit us. Yes, "a body You have prepared for Me."

Parenthetically, I have always been a bit amused at why some have a problem believing in the virgin birth and yet have no problem believing in the miracle of natural birth. How can two tiny specks of protoplasm be joined together resulting in all the intricacies of a nervous system, a respiratory system, a circulatory system and a digestive system? It is a miracle. Why, then, if we believe this can we not believe that this same great God could have planted His own seed in the womb of a young virgin girl?

Seven hundred years before Bethlehem the prophet Isaiah talked about a sign that would come. He said, "The Lord Himself will give you a sign: Behold, the virgin shall conceive and bear a son, and shall call His name Immanuel" *(Isaiah 7:14).* A sign is something that gets your attention and then tells you something. We have all seen them on the roadside during car trips. Isaiah told us to watch for a sign regarding the coming Messiah. And the sign was to be that a virgin would conceive and bear a son. This would take a miracle. So our Lord, backstage in heaven, says, "A body you have prepared for Me." God planted that seed in that virgin girl Himself.

There are those today who contend that the virgin birth is not an important Christological doctrine. But it is vitally essential to Christ's own Messiahship. He was the "God-man" and not God and man. He is God because He is the "only begotten of the Father" and He is man because He is "born of a woman." God clothed Himself in human flesh.

Yes, in the words of our Lord this Christmas Eve, "A body you have prepared for Me." What amazing condescension. He did not come as a grown man and rush out to the cross, but as a baby so that He could say to any and all of us, "I understand." He knew what it was to face the accusations of illegitimacy throughout His life. He knew what it was to be deserted by much of His family and to be betrayed by His best friends. He knew the pain of being falsely and unjustly accused.

Yes, what amazing condescension. "A body You have prepared for Me." He took a physical body so that one day we might have

a spiritual body. He came to be with us in order that one day we could go to be with Him. He became what we are that we might one day become what He is in the sense of being with Him in a glorified state in His perfect paradise. In short, He came to earth so that we could go to heaven.

The miracle of Christmas and the virgin birth is that God formed the Christ in Mary. Before the day of Pentecost one body had contained the Lord Jesus but since then all bodies can through the new birth. Paul, the apostle, said, "I labor in birth again until Christ is formed in you" *(Galatians 4:19)*.

On this Christmas Eve amid all the joy of the season, look back-stage a moment. There is a word of condescension. "A body You have prepared for Me."

A   W O R D   O F   C O M P R E H E N S I O N

"...I have come...to do Your will, O God." (Hebrews 10:5-7)

Our Lord not only comprehended the will of the Father, He came to perform it. This is the primary purpose of His advent, that is, to do the Father's will. He began with it here on Christmas Eve in heaven and thirty-three years later He ended with it in Gethsemane's garden praying, "Not My will but Yours be done" *(Luke 22:42)*. Here was a conscious willingness on His part. He willingly, voluntarily, laid down His life in obedience to the Father's will. Later, in the prime of life, He was beaten

almost beyond recognition, stripped and mocked, slapped and spit upon and finally nailed to a Roman cross of execution. And, all willingly.

Listen to our Lord, "I have come to do Your will, O God." Willingly the Lord Jesus took a body. Willingly He was led before Caiaphas, then Pilate and on to the cross. He was never dragged or pushed as an unwilling victim. Hear Him in Isaiah's prophecy, "I was not rebellious nor did I turn away. I gave my back to those who struck Me, and My cheeks to those who plucked out My beard. I did not hide My face from shame or spitting" *(Isaiah 50:5-6)*. Yes, we have a word of comprehension on this Christmas Eve. "I have come to do Your will, O God."

In the preceding verse from our text, the writer of Hebrews had said, "For it is not possible that the blood of bulls and goats could take away sins" (Hebrews 10:4). In fact He says, "Sacrifice and offering You did not desire" *(Hebrews 10:5)*. Why then all the animal sacrifices on Temple Mount? They were all pointing to the Lamb of God Himself, our Lord Jesus Christ. God took no pleasure in the sacrifice of these animals *(Hebrews 10:6)*. They all simply were pointing to Jesus. In what sacrifice then did the Father take pleasure? The final and complete sacrifice of His Son. We know this because He told us so at the baptism of the Lord by John the Baptist. John said, "Behold the Lamb of God who takes away the sin of the world" *(John 1:29)*. The Father responded from heaven saying, "This is my beloved Son, in Him I am well pleased" *(Matthew 3:17)*.

There are two small but very important words in our Lord's word of comprehension. Note carefully, He said, "I have come

to do Your will, O God." It is not simply enough for us to know the will of God. We must do it in our own experience. The Lord did not come to find the will of God. He came *to do* the will of God. And there is a huge difference in the two. Many find God's will but few seem to "do it." True success in life is not simply to find God's will for our lives but to actually do it. Jesus said, "I have come *to do* Your will, O God."

This will of the Father took Jesus to Bethlehem, to Egypt, to Nazareth, to Capernaum, to Jerusalem and on to Gethsemane, Golgotha, the grave and then back to glory. And because of His faithfulness to the Father's will, the writer of Hebrews says, "By that will we have been sanctified by the offering of the body of Jesus Christ once for all. And every priest stands ministering daily and offering the same sacrifices which can never take away sins. But this Man, after He had offered one sacrifice for sins forever, sat down at the right hand of God" *(Hebrews 10:10-12).*

What if our Lord had called those legions of angels to deliver Him from the cross? What if He had known the will of the Father but not done it? There would be no Christmas tree, no ornaments, no presents, no Christmas Eve. There would be no church steeples, no churches, no New Testament. There would be no hymns, no hope. But thanks be to God that we "know the grace of our Lord Jesus Christ, that though He was rich, yet for our sakes He became poor, that we through His poverty might become rich" *(2 Corinthians 8:9).*

There is not only a word of condescension but also a word of comprehension. The Lord came primarily to do the

Father's will and that will eventually took Him to a Roman cross. Early on He declared, "My food is to do the will of Him who sent Me and to finish His work" *(John 4:34).*

Christmas Eve in heaven. What a thought. What a night. Just before the curtain rises, our Lord turns to the Father and says, "A body You have prepared for me...I have come to do Your will, O God." Should we do less this Christmas season? Since our Lord humbled Himself to say, "A body You have prepared for Me," should we not also humble ourselves before Him? Since our Lord declared that He had come "to do" the Father's will should we do less?

On this Christmas Eve in the midst of family and friends, pageants and plays and gadgets and gifts may we sincerely join the Apostle Paul in exclaiming, "Thanks be unto God for His unspeakable gift" *(2 Corinthians 9:15).*

GuideStone·
Financial Resources

ABOUT   GUIDESTONE
FINANCIAL   RESOURCES

Dallas-based GuideStone Financial Resources is a leading financial services provider of retirement, investment and life and health plans. Operating as a church benefits board, the multi-billion dollar organization is dedicated to providing outstanding products and high-touch customer service to Southern Baptist and other evangelical churches, ministries and institutions.

GuideStone offers a wide array of retirement services including retirement and executive compensation plans, personal and institutional investment products and recordkeeping services. Christian-based, socially screened investment programs utilize a sophisticated manager-of-managers philosophy.

Life and Health products made available through GuideStone include a variety of term life, accident, disability, medical and dental plans with a wide range of benefit options.

Founded in 1918 as a relief organization, GuideStone continues its tradition of providing financial assistance to retired Southern Baptist ministers and ministers' widows with insufficient retirement income. For more information about GuideStone's products, services and endowment opportunities, visit *www. GuideStone.org* or call toll-free at **1-888-98-GUIDE.**